Reformation of Character

ISBN: 978-0-9914823-0-6 (paper)

Nur Publications
Union City, CA
United States of America
www.nurpublications.org

Library of Congress Control Number
2014942475

First edition: September 2010
Second edition: June 2012
Third edition: June 2017

Design, Editing & Cover by: Nur Publications

Printed in the United States of America

Reformation OF CHARACTER

Hadrat Mawlānā Shāh Hakīm Muhammad Akhtar Sahib

Translated by Mawlānā Tameem Ahmadi

Nur Publications

2017

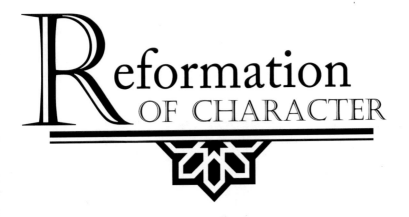

Dedication

All of my writings and compilations are collections of the benefits and blessings from the companionship of our spiritual mentors:

Muḥyī al-Sunnah Ḥaḍrat Aqdas Mawlānā Shāh Abrār al-Ḥaqq Ṣāḥib ﷺ

Ḥaḍrat Aqdas Mawlānā Shāh ʿAbd al-Ghanī Ṣāḥib Phūlpūrī ﷺ

Ḥaḍrat Aqdas Mawlānā Shāh Muḥammad Aḥmad Ṣāḥib ﷺ

-Muḥammad Akhtar
(May Allah pardon him)

TABLE OF CONTENTS

Foreword

BY MUFTI ZUBAIR BAYAT
RECTOR OF DARUL IHSAN ISLAMIC SERVICES CENTER
& SPIRITUAL DEPUTY OF THE AUTHOR

OUR HONOURABLE SPIRITUAL MENTOR, ʿĀrifbillah Mawlānā Shāykh Ḥakīm Muḥammad Akhtar of Karachi was not only a *ḥakīm* (herbal doctor) of physical illnesses, but he was in fact a 'super specialist' of diagnosing and treating spiritual illnesses. Thousands acquired cure through his expert treatment and not only were they cured, but some even qualified under his mentorship to become spiritual 'doctors', who are now dispensing the remedies and prescriptions acquired from their Shaykh and mentor. The spiritual 'illnesses' and maladies that these spiritual 'doctors' treat are relating to the soul and heart of man, and are manifested in the character and conduct of people. If a person is spiritually 'sick', then sickening conduct and behavior is displayed by such a person. If on the other hand, a person is spiritually 'well' and 'healthy', excellent and exemplary conduct is displayed. So a spiritual 'doctor' is concerned about the removal of spiritual illnesses, that must be replaced by spiritual wellbeing. This wonderful book, titled REFORMATION OF CHARACTER, written by our Shaykh, is in fact a concise manual dealing with this very subject matter. Due to its brevity it makes for easy reading and reference, and serves as an excellent primer and introduction to this much neglected facet of every Muslim's life. Such is the state of ignorance and indifference about spiritual 'health' that the vast majority of Muslims do not even realise the state of the spiritual 'ill health', which is not only disastrous in the life of this world, but even more calamitous in the next life. Allah save us all. May Allah reward our brother, a dynamic young scholar, Mawlānā Shaykh Tameem Ahmed for rendering this most useful and vital book from its original Urdu, into lucid and flowing English, so that a countless number of English speaking people from all the world can derive benefit from it. May Allah accept the noble efforts of the illustrious author, as well as the translator and reward them abundantly in both worlds.

(MUFTI) ZUBAIR BAYAT
DURBAN, SOUTH AFRICA

بسم الله الرحمن الرحيم

A Brief Life-Sketch of the Author

Ḥaḍrat Mawlānā Shāh Ḥakīm Muḥammad Akhtar Ṣāḥib (May Allah have mercy on him)

The lover and knower of Allah, the shaykh of shaykhs, the Rūmī of his time, Ḥaḍrat Mawlānā Shāh Ḥakīm Muḥammad Akhtar was born in 1927 in a small village in India called Athiya, in the Uttar Pradesh District of Partabgarh.

He was the only son - accompanied by two sisters - of a hard-working father and dedicated mother. Even as a child, he showed a God-given affinity towards piety and righteousness. His earliest memories, even in his infancy, were of being carried by his older sister to the local Imām of his masjid, who would bless him and pray for him. Ḥaḍrat, quite affectionately, remembered the Imām's beard and white, shining clothes. Even at that tender age, Ḥaḍrat felt drawn to and had a deep connection with the people of piety.

At the age of twelve, Ḥaḍrat would come to know the name of this local Imām, Ḥāfiẓ Abul-Barakāt, and would learn that he was a disciple and *khalīfah* (spiritual deputy) of Ḥakīm al-Ummah, Mawlānā Ashraf ʿAlī Thānwī. Upon realizing the qualifications and scholarly pedigree of his beloved Imām, he immediately requested initiation into the precise spiritual path that the Imām was engaged in, and, further requested that he personally grant him spiritual guidance as well. Ḥāfiẓ Abul-Barakat, however, respectfully declined both propositions. "Ḥakīm al-Ummah granted me *khilāfah* to guide and assist laypersons and the general public, not the elite," the Imām explained. "You are not a layperson and you will soon be initiated by someone who is a very special servant of Allah."

While still a pre-teen, Ḥaḍrat had resolved to routinely frequent an abandoned masjid in the middle of the jungle in the city of Sulṭānpūr, where his family had resided briefly. There, he would offer the night prayers and cry out of adoration in the love of Allah Taʿālā[1] until the break of dawn. He would return home only after performing the Fajr prayers. The villagers in close proximity to the masjid had, for the most part, left their religious obligation to pray; however, inspired by the constancy of this young adolescent, they became encouraged and motivated to attend the prayers.

1. An Arabic and Urdu phrase of exaltation of Allah ﷻ, meaning, "Most High", or "Most Exalted

Needless to say, the remote masjid became lively again after many years of heedlessness.

Shortly after completing elementary school, Ḥaḍrat implored his father to allow him admission into Dār al-ʿUlūm Deoband, the premier *madrasah* of its time in India. His father promptly declined the request and, instead, enrolled him into secular middle school. Ḥaḍrat, dutifully – albeit with a solemn heart – fulfilled his father's request.

But his ardent desire to pursue the sacred sciences of *Sharīʿah* would not take a back seat forever. After completion of middle-school, he eagerly commenced his preliminary Islamic studies with the Imām and *khaṭīb* of Sulṭānpūr Jāmiʿ Masjid, Mawlānā Qārī Muḥammad Ṣiddīq. There, he studied Farsi and beginners' books such as *Karīmāh, Bostān, and Gulistān*. However, his father interrupted his studies again and required of him to take admission into Tibbiyya College in Ilāhabād, to pursue the study of herbal medicine. This entreaty from his father came with the permission, however, that upon the completion of his herbal medicine course at Tibbiyya College, Ḥaḍrat would be free to seek enrollment into the *madrasah* of his choice.

Tibbiyya College turned out to be a source of great benefit for the young man. It was at this point on his spiritual journey that he met a great lover of Allah, a Naqshbandī Shaykh and the *khalīfah* of Mawlānā Fazl al-Raḥmān Ganj-Murādabādī,

Ḥaḍrat Mawlānā Shāh Muḥammad Aḥmad Ṣāḥib. He studied with him for three years and benefited from him immensely. Moreover, he enthusiastically seized the opportunity to attend the daily *dhikr* gatherings of his Shaykh and was able to then quench his burning thirst for the love of Allah.

Ḥaḍrat relates, "While my class-fellows, after college, would go to watch the Hindu women bathe at the Jamna River, I would go straight to the *dhikr* gatherings of Mawlānā Shāh Muḥammad Aḥmad Ṣāḥib..." From five o'clock in the late afternoon till eleven o'clock at night, Ḥaḍrat would remain in this blessed gathering that consisted of poetry in love of Allah, advice, and heartfelt admonitions for the seekers of Allah.

It was also at this stage of his life that Ḥaḍrat sought a formal connection to a spiritual mentor and guide. He fell upon a transcribed lecture of Ḥakīm al-Ummah titled, "Contentment of the Hearts," which evoked in his heart a strong desire to make *bayʿah* (oath of commitment) and take the spiritual path with Ḥakīm al-Ummah. He thus began correspondence with him, but, unfortunately, the great Shaykh was not able to continue replying to Ḥaḍrat's letters due to an extreme illness and the physical frailty resulting from it. The Shaykh's deputy, Mawlānā Shabbīr ʿAlī Thānwī, advised Ḥaḍrat to seek a spiritual mentor from among Ḥakīm al-Ummah's *khalīfahs*. This was when Ḥaḍrat chose to connect himself with Mawlānā Shāh ʿAbd al-Ghanī Phūlpūrī.

He finally completed his course at Tibbiyya College and gained admission into the *madrasah* of his Shaykh, Madrasah Bayt al-ʿUlūm in Saray-Mīr, which was established by the consultation and supervision of Ḥakīm al-Ummah himself.

His Shaykh, Mawlānā Shāh ʿAbd al-Ghanī Phūlpūrī, was a transcendental figure, a remnant of the past – of a glorious by-gone era of illustrious Shaykhs. His humble abode was situated in a jungle, many kilometers away from the *madrasah* where he served in the capacity of principal and teacher. There were no modern facilities associated with comfort nearby, such as lavatories, bathrooms, running water, or electricity. When the need for water would arise, whether in winter or summer, Shaykh's loyal student and spiritual disciple (Ḥaḍrat) would walk one kilometer down an unpaved road to fetch water from a pond, which would completely dry up in the hot summer months.

Along with being an ardent lover of Allah and annihilated in His devotion, Ḥaḍrat's Shaykh, Shāh ʿAbd al-Ghanī, was a sturdy warrior of a man – having been duly trained in Greco-Roman wrestling and the Indian martial art of stick-fighting. His rigorous daily routine of worship would start at three in the morning; he would begin with the nightly vigil – with extended, prolonged *rakāʿahs* of *tahajjud*, recitation of the Quran, salutations on the Prophet – and continue up to ten in the morning. In intervals amidst his recitation of the Quran, he would uncontrollably cry out the name of Allah. Ḥaḍrat himself would say, "It seemed like if he did not let out Allah's name, his chest would burst out of the pressure building up inside... like steam emitting from a locomotive."

All the while, Ḥaḍrat would sit at a distance in the masjid, so as to not disturb his Shaykh's devotions. He would sit, observing him closely and connecting his own heart with the spirit of his mentor, being watchful of any need that may arise for him. When his mentor would be leaving the masjid to refresh his ablutions for the morning prayer, Ḥaḍrat would put the Shaykh's sandals before his feet. This display of eagerness and *adab* (etiquette) by the young disciple would cause the Shaykh to become very delighted.

The Shaykh customarily refrained from partaking of any breakfast or food until one o'clock. Likewise, his disciple, out of shame and *adab*, would also refrain from doing so – despite severe pangs of hunger. Even though Ḥaḍrat had been permitted by his Shaykh to eat, he could not find comfort in the thought of executing such an action if his mentor was not doing it. Thus, his youth was spent harvesting sustenance from spiritual food more so than provisions offered elsewhere. This not only sufficed him, but also nourished him and strengthened his soul for the work that he was destined for.

Commensurate with the station of the elite scholars who are acquainted with spiritual realities and are keen on sacrificing for the love and enjoyment of their Lord, he continued to climb the ladder of the spiritual sciences in the auspicious company of his Shaykh. Ḥaḍrat also continued his studies of the sacred sciences of *Sharīʿah* at his Shaykh's *madrasah*, even though he had the opportunity to study at the prestigious Dār al-ʿUlūm Deoband. Despite the censure and disapproval of his contemporaries, Ḥaḍrat gave precedence to the *ṣuḥbah* (company) of his Shaykh; yet, he was not deprived of the scholarship of great *ʿulamā'*.

Some of the reputable scholars he studied under were:

-Mawlānā ʿAbd al-Qayyūm Ṣāḥib, who was a graduate of Deoband, under whom Ḥaḍrat studied the *Mishkāt al-Maṣābīḥ*, *Tafsīr al-Jalalayn* and other texts with.

-Mawlānā Muḥammad Muslim Ṣāḥib Jawnpūrī, under whom he studied the *Saḥīḥ Muslim.*

-Mawlānā Shāh ʿAbd al-Ghanī Phūlpūrī, his Shaykh, under whom he studied the *Saḥīḥ al-Bukhārī* and the *Mathnawī Sharīf* of Mawlānā Rūmī.

He had attained such an in-depth knowledge of the *Mathnawī* that when he wrote his commentary on it, titled *Maʿārif-e-Mathnawī*, and sent a copy to illustrious scholars such as Mawlānā Yūsuf Binori and Shaykh al-Ḥadīth Mawlānā Muḥammad Zakariyyah, they praised the work tremendously. Mawlānā Binori said, "I see no difference between your Farsi poetry and Mawlānā Rūmī, and after reading your *Maʿārif-e-Mathnawī*, such a love and respect has come into my heart for you that I cannot express it in words."

For seventeen years Ḥaḍrat remained in the company of his Shaykh; until the Shaykh drew his last breath. He encountered and tolerated great hardships in his service. Ḥaḍrat would often recount that the hardships he underwent in the company and service of his spiritual mentor were so arduous that the students of today would not be able to endure a single day of such adversity: the burning envy and enmity of other students, death-threats, hunger, thirst, and poverty were just some of the obstacles he faced on his path. But these obstacles were no impediment for the one who had the sincere passion and thirst to attain the love of Allah, the one whose heart had been enlightened with the light of Allah's love. Ḥaḍrat's struggle, hardship, and sincere sacrifice rewarded him with great spiritual effulgence. He thus became a living example of what was uttered by the Knower of Allah, Imām Ibn ʿAṭā'illāh al-Iskandarī, who said, "Whoever does not have a burning beginning, will never have a shining end."

After the death of his first mentor, Ḥaḍrat connected himself to another illustrious *khalīfah* and shining star of Ḥakīm al-Ummah; in fact, the youngest deputy of Ḥaḍrat Thānwī, Mawlānā Shāh Abrār al-Ḥaqq Ṣāḥib Hardoi. He remained in his service and supervision for forty years and received *ijāzah* and *khilāfah* (permission to initiate and provide mentorship on the spiritual path) from him. The position of *mashīkhah* (spiritual-mentorship) was now officially taken up by Ḥaḍrat. This made it possible for thousands of seekers of Allah from various nationalities and all walks of life to garner benefit from him and quench their thirst for the love of Allah.

A lover of Allah, erudite scholar, brilliant poet, prolific author, rector and principle of Jāmiʿah Ashraf al-Madāris in Karachi, founder and spiritual-caretaker of Khānqah Imdādiyyah Ashrafiyyah in Karachi, Shaykh of Shaykhs and spiritual guide, Ḥaḍrat continued to serve the *dīn* of Allah until he was overcome by a stroke in May of 2000. Though the stroke left the right side of his body paralyzed, it did not make him falter in serving the *dīn* and guiding Allah's seekers.

He continued to attend his *majālis* (spiritual gatherings). He would be present in the *khānqah* four to five times a day, despite his weakness and physical frailty. We can unequivocally say that he was a mountain of resolution and had complete reliance on and contentment in the decree of Allah. He refrained from complaining about his condition; rather, he was always seen smiling and attending to his disciples, showing them love – at times showing them more love than their own parents. One can say that this stage of his life was a time of great spirituality and tremendous descent of subtle blessings from Allah. Those who attended his gatherings during this time most definitely left spiritually rejuvenated, taking with them the fervor of guidance and motivation.

In 2013, as his sickness intensified, his wished more than anything else to die on the same day as his beloved Prophet ﷺ did; this is what the burning heart of this lover yearned for. Regarding this, Ḥakīm al-Ummah once remarked, "Death on Friday is the death of the penitent, and death on Monday is the death of the lovers." His beloved Lord granted him this wish and he finally set journey to the abode of the hereafter on the eve of Monday, 23rd of Rajab, 1434, corresponding to the 2nd of June, 2013.

Ḥaḍrat's funeral in Karachi was attended by thousands of people and, beyond that, he was equally mourned by thousands of scholars, lovers and seekers of Allah who were inspired by his knowledge, practice and embodiment of the teachings of the Quran and Sunnah. May Allah shower His choicest mercies upon him and elevate his rank in Paradise. May Allah grant us the ability to follow in his footsteps and may He unite us under His Glorious Throne on the Day of Judgment. Āmīn.

بسم الله الرحمن الرحيم

Introduction

ALLAH, ﷻ STATES, “Successful is the one who has purified his *nafs* (soul) and unsuccessful is the one who does not purify it [due to laziness and neglect].”[2] Ḥakīm al-Ummah has stated that the *tazkiyah* (purification) of the *nafs* is obligatory on each individual (*farḍ ʿayn*). He further stated that the verb derived from *tazkiyah* is transitive (*fiʿl mutaʿaddī*), meaning that it requires both a subject - the purifier - and its object - the purified. Also, since it is transitive, we can establish that *tazkiya*, as an action, cannot be completed without the presence of the both of these (unlike the intransitive form - *fiʿl lāzim* - which does not require the conjunction of both the

2. Quran 91:9–10

doer of the action and the object being acted upon). Thus, the transitive verb sentence itself requires that there be someone who will facilitate the *tazkiyah* and *tarbiyah* (nurturing).

From this special feature of the verb, and from the fact that no person in and of himself can truly reform himself, we can reasonably conclude that there is always a need for a spiritual guide to facilitate this specific action. Now, it must also follow that if the prerequisite of the obligatory act (in this case, *tazkiyah*) is itself obligatory, it would make it obligatory for us to seek out that spiritual guide needed for attaining this *tazkiyah*.

But in seeking this guide, we must consider the fact that we have to be able to recognize good and evil characteristics in a person – so as to discern. This, obviously, entails that we have to have the requisite knowledge of both praiseworthy characteristics (*akhlāq ḥamīdah*) and evil characteristics (*akhlāq radhīlah*). The absence of this knowledge, conversely speaking, can have the dangerous effect of regarding evil as good and good as evil. For example, some people spend years with saintly individuals, but, since they were not able to acquire from them the ability to discern evil characteristics and sicknesses of the heart, they unfortunately remain unmindful and unconcerned about their own reformation.

It was precisely for this reason that a sincere friend, Mawlānā Muḥammad Zubayr Ṣāḥib, requested this lowly one to compile a concise book on praiseworthy and evil character, a book which would also be easy to distribute among friends. Due to the sincerity of Mawlānā, Allah ﷻ granted this lowly one the ability to compile this book entitled, *Iṣlāḥ-e-Akhlāq* (Reformation of Character). May Allah ﷻ, out of His mercy, accept it and make it beneficial for all. *Āmīn*!

(Ḥadrat Mawlānā Ḥakīm) Muḥammad Akhtar
(May Allah have mercy on him)

"Ask the People of the Remembrance —
— if you do not know..."

(al-Naḥl:43)

Statements of Ḥakīm al-Ummah Thānwī

(May Allah have mercy on him)

THE ESSENCE OF THE PATH OF SULŪK is to remove evil character and inculcate noble character, to remove heedlessness of Allah and to inculcate attention to Allah.

On Noble Character

The reality of noble character is that we must not cause any form of difficulty or inconvenience to anyone, neither outwardly nor inwardly – either in his presence or in his absence.[3]

3. Kamālāt-e-Ashrafiyyah, p. 93 §440.

For example, if we know that by practicing upon some form of optional act of *taqwa* (piety) someone's heart will be broken, then we base our practice on the *fatwa* (verdict of the scholars) instead. They have said that on such occasions, such an optional act of piety is not permissible (e.g., if by accepting a certain gift, there is disgrace for you but honor for your brother, then give preference to his honor over yours).[4]

ON EVIL CHARACTER

It is not sufficient to simply withhold oneself from causing hurt or annoyance to someone; rather, one must make a *firm resolve in the heart* to never be a cause of annoyance. The absence of this firm resolution is not sufficient[5]

REFORMATION OF CHARACTER

The Messenger of Allah ﷺ said, "Noble character dissolves sins just as salt dissolves ice, and evil character destroys worship just as vinegar destroys honey[6]." He also stated, "The most beloved to me and the one closest to me in the

4. Ibid. p. 93 §442.

5. The reason this is not sufficient is because leaving the *nafs* idle and void of this firm resolve will cause it to become negligent of others' rights.

6. Narrated by Ṭabarānī on the authority of Ibn Abbās

Hereafter will be the one whose character is good; and the one most disliked by me, and the furthest away from me in the Hereafter, will be the one whose character is evil."[7] Moreover, the Messenger of Allah ﷺ had this to say about the difference between good and bad character: "He who is deprived of softness has been deprived of all goodness."[8]

7. Narrated by Aḥmad on the authority of Tha'laba al Khushānī
8. Narrated by Tirmidhī on the authority of Abū Dardā.

"*Prosperous is he ——— who has purified himself*"

(al-Aʿlā:14)

PART 1

Noble Character

TAWBA - REPENTANCE

ʿAbdullah b. Masʿūd said, "The deep sorrow and regret one feels due to sin, is *tawba*."[9]

Let us try to understand this in a simpler way: When someone wrongs a person of prominence, then to what lengths does he go to excuse himself? He will clasp the man's hands, fall to his feet, humble himself, speak words of flattery, and even weep if need be. Likewise, when seeking repentance in front of Allah, we should adopt similar behavior; after all,

9. This statement is actually a Ḥadīth narrated by ʿAbdullah b. Masʿūd directly from the Prophet: "Feeling regretful is repentance." Narrated by Ibn Mājah, Aḥmad and al-Ṭabarānī.

He is of the highest prominence. According to His promise, *tawba* of this nature is definitely accepted!

To attain this ability to repent, you have to ponder over the punishments mentioned in the Quran and Ḥadīth. This contemplation will, undoubtedly, result in the heart beginning to dislike sin. Starting today, establish a daily regimen that includes verbal repentance and making up any (*qaḍā*) prayers and fasts that were missed heretofore. Furthermore, if you have not given a person his due right, or given an inheritor his or her inheritance, then – after consultation with the respective ʿ*ulamā*' (religious scholars) – do so. If, on the other hand, you do not have the ability to do this, then you must assuredly ask those people for forgiveness.

KHAWF - FEAR

It is narrated that Muʿādh b. Jabal ﷺ said, "The heart of a believer cannot be without fear, and his fear can never become tranquil." The method of acquiring this is to be in constant remembrance of the fact that Allah ﷻ – at all times – knows all of our actions and statements, and is fully aware of our outer and inner secrets. In addition to this – an as a sobering reminder – He will take our reckoning regarding these on the Day of Judgment.

RAJĀ' - HOPE

Allah ﷻ states, "Verily, those who are despondent of Allah's mercy are the disbelievers."[10] This shows that having hope in Allah's mercy is part of *Imān* (faith). Fortunately, we are able to acquire this hope by being obedient to Allah ﷻ, worshiping Him, and using our courage to abstain from any disobediene of Him (sins). The natural and desired consequence of this is a heart strengthened by gaining hope in the One we are obedient to, instead of having it become afraid and despondent through disobedience.

The meaning of having hope in Him, in terms of repentance, is that we should look to Allah's unlimited mercy and be absolutely convinced that our *tawba* will be accepted. Just as small sticks of dynamite have the ability to blow up mountains, how much more power must there be in Allah's mercy, a mercy by which mountains of sins break up into small bits? But this is not to say that we become accustomed to sin just because we have resolve in Allah's power to forgive those sins. This is in and of itself a dangerous deception and something worth avoiding. No one places his hand in a fire simply because he trusts the ability of a lotion to remedy whatever burns he may suffer from that fire.

10. Quran 12:87

ḤAYĀ' - MODESTY

Ḥayā' is a very beautiful quality. When someone has a sense of modesty and shame in the presence of other people, then he will be disinclined to do any act that they dislike. Similarly, if we develop shame before Allah ﷻ, our disinclination will force us to abstain from actions that the Creator dislikes. This modesty can be attained simply by allowing ourselves to sit in solitude for a stipulated period of time. In this solitude, we should reflect on our sins and disobedience to Allah ﷻ and compare them to the favors that Allah has bestowed on us, in spite of our deficiencies otherwise. After a few days of reflection and introspection, shame will undoubtedly be inculcated in the heart, and we will feel the burn of this shame in regards to disobeying Allah ﷻ.

تصدق اپنے خدا کے جاؤں یہ پیار آتا ہے مجھ کو انشاء

اِدھر سے ایسے گناہ پیہم اُدھر سے وہ دمبدم عنایت

May I be sacrificed for my Lord,
I have fallen in love with His doings;
From my side I remain in sin,
And yet, He remains bestowing His favors

Hence, it is only through the methodical penetration of shame into the heart that we are able to abstain from sin.

SHUKR - GRATITUDE

Shukr is of two types: (1) *Shukr* to Allah ﷻ, (2) *Shukr* to the creation by the means of which we have attained a bounty.

The Messenger of Allah ﷺ said, "Whosoever is not grateful to people, then he has not been grateful to Allah ﷻ."[11] This teaches us that being grateful and respectful to one's parents, teachers, spiritual guide, and all other benefactors is part of being grateful to Allah ﷻ. He further states in another ḥadīth, "If a person receives anything, if he has the ability to give a gift in place of the one received, he should do so. If, however, he is not able to, then he should at least praise the giver; thereupon, gratitude will be fulfilled. But if he conceals it – does not show appreciation – then he has exhibited ungratefulness."[12]

The reality of *shukr* is to appreciate a bounty. When one appreciates the bounty, he also appreciates the giver of that bounty. This is how gratitude to the Creator and creation is fulfilled.

However, more important than the verbal manifestation of this *shukr* is the practical application of it — to not disobey your true Master who bestows favors upon you, and to make a full effort to be obedient to Him. Only through this are we able to also fulfill the rights of our parents, teachers and shaykh. Allah has promised in the Quran an increase in

---

11.   Narrated by Aḥmad on the authority of Abū Saʿīd al-Khudrī ؓ

12.   Narrated in *al-Adab al-Mufrad* on the authority of Jābir b. ʿAbdullah ؓ

bounties to those who are thankful for those bounties. Thus, the perfection of *shukr*, lies in both doing good actions and abstaining from sins, which also includes the act of repentance and seeking forgiveness for shortcomings. Essentially, gratitude serves a dual purpose: to make us happy upon receiving the bounties of Allah ﷻ, and, consequently, build His love in our hearts. Then, through this love, enthusiasm is engendered, an enthusiasm born of the realization that He grants us so many bounties – bounties for which we should show more gratitude and worship Him in abundance. Conversely, to disobey such a Benefactor would be a great shame!

This *shukr* is acquired only though contemplation, reflecting upon the bounties of Allah ﷻ. Hence, we should specify a time for this every day and resolve to never miss it. This is referred to as *murāqabah al-inʿāmāt al-ilāhiyyah* (contemplation of the Divine bounties). We should, furthermore, be cognizant of the fact that thousands of these bounties from Allah are raining down upon us at all times. And, we should even contemplate that the calamities that befall us are indeed beneficial – in so much as they are just a bounty in disguise.

FULFILLING PROMISES

Allah ﷻ states, "O believers, fulfill your verbal agreements.[13] Verily one will be questioned regarding his pacts." This means

13. Quran 5:1

that on the Day of Judgment we will be asked, "Did you fulfill your pledges and promises or not?" Not fulfilling promises with others is a sign of hypocrisy, as is mentioned in a ḥadīth. However, if one has promised something which is contrary to the *Sharīʿah*, then it is not correct to fulfill it.

ṢABR - PATIENCE

It is narrated in *Mustadrak* that ʿAbdullah b. Masʿūd 🙵 stated, "Patience is half of faith." And Allah 🙵 states, "Verily Allah is with those who exercise patience."[14] What this means is that man has two forces within himself: one encourages him to remain firm on the *dīn* (religion), the other encourages him to chase after his desires. Essentially, *Ṣabr* refers to letting the former force dominate over the latter. *Sabr* is attained through not acting on the demands of the *nafs* (lower self), through strengthening our resolve to resist the temptations of the *nafs*. This strength associated with *ṣabr* is created by the remembrance of Allah 🙵, companionship with the friends of Allah 🙵 (*awliyāʾ*), and contemplation over death, the grave, and *Jahannam* (the Hellfire). In short, patience refers to binding the *nafs* to the matters allowed in the *dīn* and not allowing it to do acts to the contrary.

---

14.   Quran 2:153

FIVE INSTANCES OF PATIENCE:

1. If one is wealthy, patience for him is that his attitude must not become spoiled. He must not forget Allah Most Exalted and he should recall death and the loneliness of the grave. He should not despise the poor, but, rather, should be kind and soft towards them.

2. One should not become lazy at the time of worship, whether it be with regards to performing *ṣalāt* or giving *zakāt*. On such occasions, three types of patience are necessary:

   - Correct your intention before the act of worship so that you are only doing it for the pleasure of Allah Most Exalted — the *nafs* should have no share in it.

   - Do not be lax while doing acts of worship. Fulfill the acts of worship wholeheartedly, with strength and courage, in accordance with the Sunnah. Try to keep your mind attentively engaged in the act.

   - After doing the act of worship, do not go about telling people about your acts of worship.

3. One should suppress the *nafs* when it desires to sin.

4. When someone causes you harm or insult, then patience – in that instance – is to remain quiet and refrain from

taking revenge. Do this by contemplating, "Today, I will forgive so that tomorrow Allah Most Exalted will forgive my sins."

5. When there is some calamity (such as sickness, loss of wealth, or the death of a close family member or friend), then patience at such a time is to refrain from uttering a word that contravenes the *Sharīʿah*. One should not have any objections against Allah Most Exalted such as saying; "Why am I being oppressed?", or, "Why was our relative given death so quickly?" Neither should anyone wail about the calamity in front of people.

However, to cry and shed tears due to natural grief, or to express your sorrow to your close friends with the intention of lessening your sorrow, is permissible. The reason for this is that, in trying to be patient by staying totally quiet and silently bearing one's grief, one could potentially cause himself to suffer some psychological disorders or heart related problems.

When faced with such situations, we should think of the reward of being patient. Think, "All of this is only for our benefit, and failing to exercise patience will not change the Divine decree (*taqdīr*), so why should I also lose out on its rewards?" Once we realize that we can receive a reward for exhibiting *sabr* during moments of sorrow, then how can it remain a sorrow? Suffice it to say that nothing happens without Allah's wish, and His wish does not occur without wisdom. It is stated in a line of poetry:

حسرت سے میری آنکھیں، آنسوں بہا رہی ہیں
دل ہے کہ ان کی خاطر، تسلیم سر کیے ہے

Due to sorrow, my eyes are shedding tears;
But for His pleasure, my heart has
completely accepted His decision.

IKHLĀṢ - SINCERITY

Whatever work of *d*īn we do, we should intend it only for the pleasure of Allah. There should be no worldly aims underlying it, nor should it be for ostentation and show – i.e., people have to see me, to recognize me as a pious person, etc. To illustrate this point of having something contrary to a completely sincere intention, we need to reflect on, for example, fasting, *wuḍū'* (ablution), and alms. We do not fast to lighten our stomach and make it feel better, because prior to that it was in pain and suffered from loss of appetite; similarly, we do not make a fresh *wuḍū'* (ablution) to attain coolness and escape from the heat; nor, do we give alms to a beggar so that a calamity maybe removed from us. Rather, we do these things for the pleasure of Allah.

When a person does any act of worship, he should cleanse his heart of every objective besides the pleasure of Allah ﷻ. The Messenger of Allah ﷺ said, "Whoever does an action for show, then on the Day of Judgment, Allah ﷻ will expose his faults."[15] He has also said, "Even a small amount of showing off is a form of shirk (polytheism)."[16]

However, to leave out a good action due to fear of showing off is also a form of *riyā'* (ostentation or showing off). Shayṭān prevents a person from doing good actions by confronting him with the fear of showing off. He places the thought in your mind that if you do a good action, it will be for show. So understand well that to leave a good action for fear of showing off is also showing off (*riyā'*), just as performing a good action to be seen by people is. Answer Shayṭān in this manner: "When our intention is not to show people, then how can it be showing off? We regard *riyā'* as evil." Then immediately involve yourself in that good action, even though some friend or relative is nearby.

Do not be concerned with the whisperings of Shayṭān. The thoughts and feelings of *riyā'* do not constitute *riyā'* as long as you do not make the intention to purposely show off. In this manner, when you immerse yourself in good actions and are not concerned with these thoughts and whisperings, Shayṭān will become powerless and go away.

15. Narrated by Aḥmad on the authority of Abū Bakrah ؓ
16. Narrated by Ibn Mājah on the authority of Muʿādh b. Jabal ؓ

Ḥājjī Imdādullah Ṣāḥib Muhājir Makkī said, "*Riyā*' does not always remain *riyā*'. In the beginning, one does an action for showing off, then it becomes a habit, and then this habit changes into ʿ*ibādah* (worship) and then *ikhlāṣ* (sincerity)." Khawāja ʿAzīz al-Ḥasan compiled this into a poem:

وہ ریا جس پر تھے زاہد طعنہ زن

پہلے عادت پھر عبادت ہو گئی

The riyā' (ostentation) due to which
people were taunting the sālik;
First was a habit then eventually it became worship.
(i.e. it no longer remained riyā')

In short, do not be concerned with that *riyā*' which comes unintentionally, and do not abstain from good deeds due to it.

MURĀQABAH - MEDITATING ON ALLAH MOST HIGH

At all times, keep in your heart the thought that Allah is fully aware of all of our conditions – be it our outward actions, our inward intentions, or the thoughts of our hearts. In relation to this, we should think: "If I do an evil action or bring evil thoughts to my heart, then Allah may punish me in this world or in the Hereafter." Thereafter we should keep in mind, while executing any act of worship, that Allah ﷻ is watching; and, as such, it is required that He should be worshipped in a beautiful manner.

Attaining this state of *murāqabah* necessitates ascribing a fixed period of time every day for the sole purpose of briefly pondering on the following: Allah ﷻ is watching me and my heart. The reality of this contemplative thought will begin to manifest after a period of time, and it will endure. It is hoped that by the will of Allah, and with the blessings of this contemplation, we are able to refrain from any action contrary to His pleasure.

CONCENTRATION WHILE RECITING THE HOLY QURAN

Upon intending to recite the Holy Quran, you should ponder over what Allah ﷻ has commanded regarding His Book: "Recite My speech to Me, and let Me see how you recite." Also, take into consideration how you attempt to recite the Quran with so much care and beauty when in front of prominent people. Now, taking into account that Allah ﷻ is certainly ever-watchful and always listening, should we not attempt to recite in the most beautiful manner every time?

A point of caution while reciting, however, is that if you become unmindful, then immediately renew this thought and refocus. Rest assured though that the heart will be able to concentrate with relative ease after practicing for some time.

CONCENTRATION IN *ṢALĀT*

Upon initiating *ṣalāt,* one should reflect: "I am standing in front of Allah ﷻ and He is watching me. It is the Day of Judgment. The Reckoning is taking place. *Jannah* and *Jahannam* are before me." Through this reflection, the heart will begin to concentrate.

This level of concentration can also be attained through intending the use of every word that is being recited – meaning that each word that emerges is meditated upon. For example, "I am now reading this word."[17] Another method is to learn the translation of whatever is being recited in the prayer. This way, whenever any word is read, one is able to think about it and ponder over its meaning.

Through these methods of reflection and concentration, a servant will come to know what he is saying to his Master and Creator. He will attain great enjoyment as he prostrates. His thoughts will be that his head is lowered, submitting before the Majesty of Allah ﷻ, as is stated in a ḥadīth, "When a believer prostrates, his head is at the feet of al-Raḥmān (The Most Merciful)."[18] *SubḥānAllah*![19] How blessed is that

17. This means to focus on each word of the prayer as you are reciting it and saying it volitionally, as opposed to rote recitation that often comes when prayer becomes a ritual habit.

18. Narrated by Imām al-Suyūṭī in *al-Jāmiʿ al-Ṣaghīr* and Saʿīd b. Manṣūr in *al-Sunan.*

19. "Glory be to Allah!"

head which is lying at the feet of his True Master. Ask the lovers of Allah about the enjoyment of realizing this!

Mawlānā Fazl-Raḥmān Ganj-Murādabādī ﷺ said to Ḥakīm al-Ummah Thānwī ﷺ, "My beloved Ashraf ʿAlī, when I place my head in prostration, it feels as though Allah ﷻ is showing love to me and He has taken me into His extreme proximity." In prostration, only the special friends of Allah ﷻ are granted such unique closeness. A poet once beautifully stated:

پر دے اٹھے ہوے بھی ہیں اُن کی اِدھر نظر بھی ہے

بڑھ کے مقدر آزما سر بھی ہے سنگِ در بھی ہے

The veils are lifted; And His gaze is in this direction;
Venture forward and test fortunate destiny,
for present is the head, as is the threshold.

Yet another way of gaining concentration in prayer is to focus attentively on each particular posture one is engaged in at the time. An example of this would be that while in the standing posture one should focus on the fact that he is in the standing posture and not think of anything else; in the bowing posture (*rukūʿ*), one should focus on bowing; and, in prostration (*sajdah*), one should focus only on the prostration. Focusing on perfecting each posture and properly transitioning from one posture to the next.

METHODS FOR ATTAINING ALLAH'S LOVE

THE 1ST METHOD – REMEMBRANCE OF ALLAH

A very easy method in attaining Allah's love is this: spending even a short period of time every day in the company of a person gradually yields to the development of a relationship. The result of two people meeting daily for a short time is that if, for some reason, they are not able to meet each other one day, they will become restless for each other's company and yearn to meet again. There is no need for proof regarding this; it is a well-established fact and understood by everyone.

Correspondingly, we should begin meeting Allah ﷻ every day for some stated period of time. This should begin with taking some prayer beads and, facing the *qibla* (direction of prayer) in solitude, invoking Allah ﷻ (*dhikr*) for a short duration. This *dhikr* is the meeting with Allah ﷻ. It should be noted that reciting any of the following constitutes *dhikr:* the statement of Divine oneness (*Lā ilāha illā Allah*—there is no god but Allah), salutations upon the Prophet ﷺ, recitation of the Holy Quran, and invoking the Blessed Name by saying "Allah, Allah".

It is narrated in a sacred ḥadīth (*ḥadīth qudsī*), "I am the companion of the one who remembers Me."[20] The significance of a *ḥadīth qudsī* is that it is a statement of the Prophet ﷺ

20. Narrated by Ibn Abī Shayba in his al-Muṣannaf and al-Bayhaqī in Shuʿab al-Imān.

wherein he relates Allah's words. By the statement, "I am the companion of" in this *ḥadīth qudsī*, Allah ﷻ is saying, "I am with him." Essentially, initiating *dhikr* allows one to meet the Creator. What an easy way for a servant to meet Allah ﷻ whenever he wants!

While walking, if one calls out or recites softly, "*Yā 'Ḥalīm, Yā Karīm, Yā Wāsiᶜ al-Maghfira* (O Clement, O Generous, O Possessor of Expansive Forgiveness)," Allah ﷻ will manifest on the servant the blessings and goodness of these names. When he says, "*Yā Ḥalīm*", then it is as though he has sought the quality of clemency. Clemency means to refrain from revenge in spite of having the ability to exact the revenge. Thus, this All-Powerful Being will not punish the sinful servant in spite of having the power to do so. When one says "*Yā Karīm,*" then it is as though he has called on the quality of *karam* (generosity). Consequently, Allah ﷻ, while withholding His punishment through His kindness, will also bestow favors upon His servant. When one says "*Yā Wāsiᶜ al-Maghfira,*" then Allah ﷻ, by His unlimited and vast quality of forgiveness, will forgive the limited sins of a sinful servant.

If we accustom ourselves to reading these words while walking, sitting and lying down, then there is hope of receiving many favors of Divine closeness. Through the blessings of this closeness, we can develop forbearance and generosity and become forgiving of the faults of others. The abundant recitation of these words is an elixir for many spiritual ailments, such as: succumbing to anger or desire to take revenge, stinginess, and not overlooking and forgiving the errors of people. This is true to such an extent that even if a person with evil character recites these words with sincerity and with the intention of reformation, then, Allah willing, he too will become a person of good character.

The 2nd Method – Pondering Over Allah's Bounties

Another method of attaining Allah's love is by contemplating over His bounties. We should reflect on the fact that He created the whole universe (including the heavens, earth, oceans, mountains, trees, animals and birds) for our benefit and nurturing, whereas He created us solely for His worship. Think of this and every other bounty, and be grateful. The logical progression for this line of thought is that natural love is fostered for the One who we see as our benefactor. It is narrated in a ḥadīth, "The hearts naturally incline towards loving those who do good to them, and they naturally hate those who do wrong to them."[21]

The 3rd Method – Company of the Lovers of Allah

The third method of attaining Allah's love — indeed, the method which serves as the soul and essence of the other two

21. Narrated by al-Bayhaqī in *Shuʿab al-Imān* on the authority of ʿAbdullah b. Masʿūd ﷺ.

methods, and which has the potential to yield most benefit — is that one should spend time in the company of the lovers of Allah; and he should listen to their talks with love and conviction. A ḥadīth states, "The heart of My close friends are the treasure-stores of *taqwā*."[22] Just as one attains gold from a gold mine, silver from a silver mine, and salt from a salt mine, the treasures of *taqwā* and the love of Allah ﷻ will only be attained through the companionship of His close friends. Jurists, in the classical texts, explain this by citing the example of the donkey that, by chance, falls to its death in a salt mine; after some time, the donkey decomposes and eventually becomes inseparable from the salt. Similarly, if you annihilate your opinion in the presence of your Shaykh, leaving aside your rank and status, and you stay with him for a few days, Allah willing, you will also become Allah's friend. Mawlānā Rūmī ؒ has stated, "If you are a stone, then do not lose hope. By going to those whose hearts are connected to Allah ﷻ, you will become a pearl."

These three methods of attaining Allah's love comprise the advice of Ḥakīm al-Ummah Thānwī ؒ, which this weak servant has written with some explanation. May Allah ﷻ grant this weak servant and all our honorable readers the treasure of His love. *Āmīn*!

22. Narrated by Ṭabarānī on the authority of ʿAbdullah b. ʿUmar ؓ

Which Servants Receive Allah's Love?

Al-Sayyid al-Imām Aḥmad al-Rifāʿī ﷺ said that, for the servant whom Allah loves, He does the following:

- He shows him his faults.
- He creates within him love and compassion for all of the creation.
- He makes his hand accustomed to spending generously.
- He grants him a special enthusiasm to host people. So virtuous is this act of worship that the Messenger of Allah ﷺ used to do it even before being tasked with the prophetic message.
- He creates great courage and determination in him as well as the ability to conceal the faults of others. He grants him such keen awareness of his own faults that he regards himself as the lowest, meekest, most unworthy among all.
- He makes him His beloved by virtue of the servant remaining on the path of humility and meekness. There is no shortage of greatness in the treasury of Allah ﷻ. Humility, on the other hand, is not found in His treasury. Allah ﷻ is free from humility because it is the quality of a slave; thus, He loves this quality in His servants.

- He removes from his heart the desire to be considered great by his fellow creation, and – furthermore – He removes from him the inclination to consider himself superior.
- He will grant him the respect of all creation because he gave due respect to Allah ﷻ.

Allah's creation is the threshold of the door of His Divine court. If you come to know the reality of respecting His creation, then the doors of acceptance by Him will open for you. On the other hand, if you continuously fight and argue with creation, then you will become embroiled with them and, ultimately, be deprived of Allah's closeness. Thus, etiquette towards creation is to take the hearts of people into consideration: always attempt to gladden them. The ones whom Allah ﷻ has granted His special closeness, and the ones who have been granted a true feeling of His recognition, are always engaged in trying to join hearts. These people have laid down their cheeks on the walkways of people. By virtue of this humility and self-annihilation, their souls have begun to fly with internal wings in the courts of Allah's acceptance!

These people have, by means of the creation, recognized Allah ﷻ. A *ḥadīth qudsī*[23] states, "I am with those people whose hearts have shattered due to My Grandeur, My Greatness, and My Majesty; and, they choose humility for

23. A *ḥadīth* wherein the Messenger ﷺ is narrating directly from Allah ﷻ

My pleasure."[24] This ḥadīth clearly shows that one should be humble and submissive in front of people. However, the objective of this should not be based on any worldly desire, but rather, only for the sake of Allah Most High.

Yet still, annihilating one's *nafs* to this level is not easy; if it was, the world would be replete with the friends of Allah ﷻ. This is a bounty that can only be attained by keeping the company of a pious and righteous elder who is an intense lover of Allah Most High. Needless to say, however, this comes at a cost: one has to strive.

مے یہ ملی نہیں ہے یوں قلب و جگر ہوئے ہیں خوں

کیوں میں کسی کو مفت دوں مے مری مفت کی نہیں

I did not receive it just like that;
My heart and liver became blood in the process.
(i.e. I worked hard for it)
Why should I give it to anyone for free;
When my efforts were not for free?

In other words, if this bounty were to be granted freely, there would be no appreciation for it. Mawlānā Rūmī رحمه الله has said:

---

24. Al-ʿAllāmah al-Munāwī writes in Fayḍ al-Qadīr (1:519) that this statement has been mentioned in the previously revealed Divine scriptures.

لیک شرینی و لذاتِ مقر

ہست بر اندازہ رنجِ سفر

The sweetness and enjoyment of the destination;
Is equal to the suffering one undergoes during one's journey.

RESPECT FOR ELDERS

It is a sign of felicity and good fortune that one has respect for his parents, teachers, and elders; that he has compassion for his juniors; and, has respect for scholars. The definition of good fortune (which is granted by Allah ﷻ) is that one has the ability to do good. Our pious and righteous elders have stated, "One who is respectful will be fortunate, but who possesses no respect will be unfortunate."

The one who is disrespectful to his elders is inviting his juniors to be disrespectful to him. The Messenger of Allah ﷺ said, "Stay chaste from other women and your women will remain chaste. Be good to your parents and your children will be good to you. If anyone asks you for forgiveness then forgive him. Whoever does not forgive others will be deprived of the Pond of *Kawthar* on the plains of Resurrection."[25]

25. Narrated by al-Ṭabarānī on the authority of Jābir b. ʿAbdullah ؓ. Al-Munāwī, Fayḍ al-Qadīr, §3139.

More specifically, to even say "*uff*"[26] to your parents is *ḥarām* (unlawful). Rights of parents are so meritorious that – for example – even if the parents of a disobedient child have passed away and he send rewards to them in great abundance, then there is hope that even he will be resurrected among the obedient children.[27]

COMPASSION FOR THE VULNERABLE

To have mercy and compassion for one's wife, children and the weak is a sign of a soft heart and good fortune. The Messenger of Allah ﷺ has said, "The best among you with regards to character is the one who has good character with his family members." How can the character of a person be noble when he keeps his friends and acquaintances happy, but upon returning home, he makes life difficult for his family – be it making his wife and children cry by becoming angry, or antagonizing them over small matters? To show good character and to show how to live amicably with one's wife, Allah ﷻ has revealed the command in the Quran: "And treat them with kindness."[28]

26. Meaning to make even the most minor sound of disgruntlement.
27. The method of "sending rewards" to the decreased is to perform an optional act of worship such as charity, recitation of the Quran, etc. Thereafter, supplicating to Allah and dedicating the rewards of that deed to the deceased. The basis of this act can be found in al-Bukhārī, ḥadīth #2762.
28. Quran 4:19

I will narrate two incidents, which with a little reflection will provide sufficient for advice.

THE FIRST INCIDENT

Some husbands are so oppressive that they neglect their wives (who leave their parents and their whole family just to come and live with their husbands). Such husbands then go and amuse themselves with others, only to come home at night to eat and then sleep. Who will cheer up such a woman who, due to the command of the *Sharīʿah*, is like a prisoner in her husband's home?

There was a husband who used to rebuke his wife for every little matter. Day and night, he would amuse himself with his friends. His wife used to wait for him all day, by herself. By chance, one day, this husband began to suffer from severe diarrhea, and he found himself continuously vomiting and defecating. Eventually he was bedridden and continued to urinate and defecate there. In his time of adversity, it was his wife who resolved to clean the feces and wash him; a task that no other friend or relative in the world sought fit to assist him in.

Now, according to the Sharīʿah, the wife is the only person qualified to clean her husband's private parts. Only the wife can fulfill this duty. A mother fulfills this duty during infancy, but, after coming of age, it is not even permissible for her to engage in this service. The lesson we derive from this is that the wife is such a bounty that she will assist even in the most difficult of times. Obviously, when the husband recovered, he called his wife and cried, "Forgive me, I have not properly appreciated you. Allah opened my eyes with this sickness. I was blind, but now I can see. From today, I will appreciate you!"

The Second Incident

There was a husband who had a careless attitude toward his wife and would keep a very distant relationship with her. He had no affection for her. On occasion, he would even hit her over small mistakes, and he had a habit of speaking harshly to her. His general temperament was melancholic—may Allah ﷻ protect us from having such a dry nature! Alas, to be a loving person is a great fortune and a great bounty.

This man's daughter got married and, subsequently, her husband began beating her. The man went to get help and began crying, "My daughter is suffering so much oppression. The husband does not care about the pain and hurt she is suffering. What else does my daughter have to go through?" A local scholar who was his old friend, said, "You used to hit your wife, leave her alone at night, and run off. You used to sit with your friends instead of pleasing her heart, either by way of speaking to her or tending to her pains and sorrows.

Now, without becoming angry, tell me clearly, was that poor one (i.e., your wife) not someone's daughter and someone's beloved? Ah! If only you could have realized it at that time! However, now you can easily understand it!"

Upon hearing this, he began crying and said, "I have oppressed my wife!" He then proceeded straight to his house and asked his wife for forgiveness. For the remainder of his life, he loved her with great compassion, love, and closeness. He began regarding every sorrow of his wife's as his own and was granted the ability to observe the etiquette of good companionship and fulfill her rights.

Taslīm, Riḍā, Tafwīḍ & Duʿā - Submission, Pleasure, Resignation of Affairs, & Supplication

Those matters in the world which are not in harmony with one's desires will, at times, cause extreme grief, sorrow, and ultimately, ill-health. This will also transition to one's religious matters, where weakness and laxity will be found as well. Allah ﷻ has, for this reason, commanded us to be content with what has been predestined. Reflect on the fact that even though something is contrary to your pleasure, it is from Allah and by His design; not even a leaf moves without Allah's will. Furthermore, consider that no harm can come from it since there is only benefit in afflictions; after all, the special mercy of Allah is much greater than even the mercy of one's own parents.

Bahlūl ﵀ was a pious and righteous elder. Someone asked him, "How are you?" He replied, "What can you ask of the condition of one according to whose desire the entire universe is running?" The person asked, "How can this be?" He answered, "In the world, all matters take place according to Allah's desire. I have annihilated my desire before His desire. Thus, whatever is the desire of my Master is my desire, and so everything is taking place according to my desire and, for that reason, I am happy in every condition!"

By this teaching of Allah ﷻ, a servant will remain happy in all conditions. There may be some sorrow and grief, but there will not be unbearable hardship. Rather, the small amount of grief associated with the hardship will only serve to increase the enjoyment that the servant experiences when he is making *duʿā* to Allah. It will also be a means of attaining a special proximity. Through this proximity one will be saved from the love of this world and will not find himself unmindful of the Hereafter. This is the lesson by which the pious servants of Allah ﷻ, in great comfort, pass their days and nights. A worldly person, however, loses his senses and begins melting over trivial matters.

The friends of Allah ﷻ, on the other hand, can withstand a mountain of sorrow; to them, it is no more than the likes of a mosquito's wing, something they send flying on the catapult of *taslīm* and *riḍā* (submission and pleasure)! The reality of *riḍā bi'l-qaḍā* (pleasure with the Divine decree) is to continue asking Allah ﷻ for goodness and to be pleased with the decision that He decrees. The servant only brings misfortune upon himself when he stops asking for goodness and he becomes displeased with Allah's decision. Being pleased with Allah ﷻ, however, does not mean that there is no sorrow and sadness in one's heart during the unfavorable circumstances. It is similar to, say, when a doctor performs an operation on the patient and there are residual scars and pain; yet, despite the pain, the patient is happy with the doctor.

What must have been the condition of Prophet Yaʿqūb ؑ who, in grief over his son Yūsuf ؑ, cried so much? However, in his heart he was pleased with the decision of Allah ﷻ and he would present his sorrows to Him alone. Khwāja Ṣāḥib ؒ explains the enjoyment of this *taslīm* (submission) in the following words,

سوگ میں یہ کس کی شرکت ہو گئی

بزمِ ماتم بزمِ عشرت ہو گئی

Who has participated in the gathering of sorrow and grief?
The gathering of sorrow and grief has become the gathering of joy and happiness

However, this bounty of being pleased with the decision of Allah will only be attained when one has love for Allah ﷻ and conviction in the Hereafter. This conviction and love of Allah ﷻ is attained by remembrance of Him (*dhikr*), worship, and the company of Allah's accepted servants. When the son of the Messenger of Allah ﷺ passed away, he said, "O Ibrahim, verily the eyes are shedding tears and the heart is grieved, but we will only say with the tongue that which pleases our Master. We are definitely saddened by your separation." When one of the *Ṣaḥāba* (a Companion) asked out of astonishment, "Do you also cry?" the Messenger of Allah ﷺ replied, "O Ibn ᶜAwf, this is a mercy (i.e., this crying is due to mercy)." When Mawlānā Qāsim Nanotwī ؒ passed away, Ḥaḍrat Gangohī ؒ was grief-stricken. He said, "If I did not have something, I would have been bedridden due to grief." People asked what that "something" was. He replied, "A connection with Allah ﷻ." May Allah ﷻ grant it to all of us. Āmīn.

Combining *Tafwīḍ* and *Duᶜā*

Some of the pious elders, due to being overtaken by certain spiritual states,[29] left out even making *duᶜā* and regarded it to be contrary to *taslīm* (submission) and *tafwīḍ* (resignation of affairs). However, Ḥakīm al-Ummah Thānwī ؒ said, "A

29. This is referring to an overwhelming spiritual state that a pious individual can be affected by.

person who is overtaken by a spiritual state is excused. He cannot be imitated. Only one who has control over himself should be imitated and followed. . ." Then he said, "Together with *taslīm* and *tafwīḍ*, the actual *Sunnah* is to supplicate. To combine them, one should continue asking Allah ﷻ for well-being, while having the intention in the heart that 'if my supplication is not accepted, I will still be pleased.'"

My *murshid* (spiritual guide), Ḥaḍrat Mawlānā Shāh Abrār al-Ḥaqq Ṣāḥib ؒ said, "A believer is successful in all conditions. That is, he continues pleasing Allah ﷻ in favorable conditions with gratitude, and in unfavorable conditions he pleases Him with patience." Mawlānā Shāh Muḥammad Aḥmad Ṣāḥib Partabgharī ؒ has so beautifully stated,

بے کیفی میں بھی ہم نے تو ایک کیفِ مسلسل دیکھا ہے

جس حال میں بھی وہ رکھتے ہیں، اس حال کو اکمل دیکھا ہے

جس راہ کو ہم تجویز کریں، اُس راہ کو اثقل دیکھا ہے

جس راہ سے وہ لے جاتے ہیں ، اُس راہ کو اسہل دیکھا ہے

We saw continuous joy even in a state of joylessness;
In whichever condition He keeps us,
we consider that condition to be the most perfect.
We found that the path which we choose for
ourselves to be the most difficult path;
But we found that the path which He leads us on
to be the easiest.

TAWAKKUL - RELIANCE

Allah ﷻ states, "Only upon Allah should the believers rely."[30] Ibn ʿAbbās ؓ narrates that the Messenger ﷺ said, "From my *Ummah* (nation), seventy thousand will enter Paradise without any reckoning. They are the people who do not use amulets, who do not believe in evil omens and have trust in their Sustainer."[31] Some narrations state, "And they do not take medication." Thus, to either use or not use medication is from the *Sunnah* because ease was prescribed for every person, weak or strong. It should be mentioned here, however, that the meaning of "people who do not use amulets" is that they do not use impermissible amulets. Regarding impermissible amulets, some have stated, "It is best not to use amulets at all." Believing in evil omens is to believe, for example, that if someone sneezes or if an animal comes in front of someone, it is bad luck and causes one to fall into unnecessary doubts. Good omens, however, are permissible.[32]

INCORRECT NOTIONS REGARDING *TAWAKKUL*

Today, some people have understood *tawakkul* (reliance) to mean the abandonment of all means and efforts, and to

30. Quran 3:160

31. Narrated by al-Bukhārī and Muslim.

32. A good omen is something that you see or hear that increases your hope in Allah, due to your good opinion of Allah.

sit idly expecting things to come to us. This understanding is completely incorrect. The *tawakkul* taught to us by the *Sharīʿah* is that we should make use of the means and avenues available to us, as if they were a begging cup, and, furthermore, believe that only Allah ﷻ is the Giver. What this signifies is that the success of our means is based on Allah's grace.

Consider the fault of logic of those who regard *tawakkul* to signify the abandonment of means for achieving a desired end: do these same people not open their mouths to eat, chew their food, or eventually swallow their food? These are, after all, the means by which food reaches its desired end, the stomach. We can see from this that the correct perspective of *tawakkul* includes understanding the relationship between means and ends.

Similarly, it is not contrary to *tawakkul* for a person to be apprehensive when his sustenance is delayed. Despite having trust in Allah's promise of providing sustenance, being naturally uneasy with the situation is nonetheless acceptable because the date, time and amount for the bounty or sustenance are never specified; ultimately, we never know when we will receive this or how much. The benefit of this is that we are granted the ability to make excessive *duʿā*. Logically, this will engender trust in Allah Most High.

"Whoever is guarded against the avarice —
— of their soul, they are the prosperous"
(al-Taghābun:16)

PART 2

Evil Character

THE CURE FOR *KIBR* - REGARDING ONESELF AS GREAT

Regarding oneself as great is a very dangerous illness. It is the same sickness that caused Shayṭān to become rejected. Since then, Shayṭān has been effortlessly inflicting people with this sickness and using it, quite effectively for that matter, in leading them astray. This sickness causes a son to fight with his father, a student with his teacher, a *murīd* (spiritual aspirant) with his Shaykh, and a slave with Allah Most High. Because of this sickness, Shayṭān not only became the first to be rejected from the Divine court, but it was also the cause of his destruction. For this reason, the pious and righteous elders tell their friends and servants to be extremely cautious of *Kibr*.

It is precisely because of this sickness that a person will regard himself to be superior to others in knowledge, worship, piety, wealth, honor, intellect, or any other matter. He will go on to regard others as lowly and despicable. This type of person is always despised by others, though they may praise him in his presence out of fear of him, or for the advancement of their own personal greedy motives. This type of person does not accept anyone's advice and, worse yet, will fight those who advise him. A person inflicted with this sickness will not even accept the truth when someone offers it to him.

The reality of *kibr* has been referred to in a ḥadīth as, "Looking down on people and rejecting the truth." Anyone who finds these two symptoms within himself should immediately seek a cure for his illness; there is a real fear that all of his good deeds may be reduced to dust if left untreated. Another ḥadīth about *kibr* states, "Whosoever has in his heart a mustard seed's worth of arrogance will not attain even the fragrance of Jannah (Paradise)", never mind Jannah itself. Moreover, The Messenger of Allah ﷺ drew a stark comparison in another ḥadīth, "Whoever humbles and lowers himself for Allah, Allah will grant him honor and status among people, even though he regards himself as lowly. He who lives with arrogance, Allah will disgrace him until he will be regarded as more despicable than a dog or a pig in the eyes of people, even though he regards himself as very great in his heart."[33]

If, on the other hand, a person does not despise anyone, but only regards himself as being good, then he regards his accomplishments and good fortunes to be products of his own perfection and not gifts from Allah ﷻ. This type of person neither fears the declination or changing of any bounty, whether it be knowledge, piety, steadfastness, spiritual exercises, worship, beauty, wealth, honor, or good character. This is referred to as *ʿujub* (conceitedness). In the *Sharīʿah*, both arrogance and conceitedness are prohibited. Regarding this, Ḥakīm al-Ummah Thānwī said in *Kamalāt-e-Ashrafīyyah*, "When a servant becomes lowly and despised in his own sight, then he is good in the sight of Allah ﷻ; and, when he regards himself to be good in his own sight, then he is evil in the sight of Allah ﷻ."

THE CURE FOR *KIBR* AND *'UJUB* - *CONCEITEDNESS*

The cure for arrogance is to reflect over Allah's greatness and to think of our own mortality, our final result. We should reflect on the reality that we do not know how our own death will be. Furthermore, we should consider that it is highly probable that Allah ﷻ may detest some of our actions so

33. Ḥakīm al-Ummah Thānwī has recorded this ḥadīth in his book Khuṭubāt al-Aḥkām.

much that He washes away all of our good deeds because of it. And, inversely, He may take the person whom we are looking down upon, and, through the blessings of a single noble act that is beloved to Allah ﷻ, forgive an entire lifetime of his sins.

Along with this, our righteous elders have mentioned an incident that will greatly assist us in curing this sickness. The local girls of a neighborhood beautified and decorated a bride as she was getting married. She looked exceptionally beautiful bedecked in her jewelry and attractive clothing. Her friends complimented her, saying, "Sister, you look gorgeous. When you go to your husband, he will really appreciate you." Upon hearing this, the girl began crying. She said, "O my friends and sisters, I do not find joy in your compliments and praises. Only when my husband sees me, likes me, and compliments me, will I be absolutely delighted."

Some pious and righteous elders, on hearing this, began sobbing and fell down unconscious. Just like the adorned bride, how could they find pleasure in people's praise without knowledge of what decision Allah ﷻ had in store for them on the Day of Judgment, when He sets His sights on them. Thus it is foolishness to regard oneself as a pious and righteous individual in this world. We should, instead, take lesson from this girl's intelligence.

Ḥaḍrat Shāh ʿAbd al-Ghanī ؒ used to say, "When our death occurs on *Imān* (faith), only then can we celebrate all the actions we had done in our life. To celebrate before that and to regard oneself as great due to people's praise is foolishness!"

The cure for ʿ*ujub* is that we should regard every excellence and bounty as a gift from Allah ﷻ. Also, we should be vigilant of and incessantly fearful of that fact that, due to some evil action of ours, these bounties can be abruptly taken away. We should be in constant fear of Allah's qualities of being above want of anything and His Self-Sufficiency – in that He does not need our worship, but that we need Him. Regarding this, our pious and righteous elders have stated, "Continue doing good deeds and at the same time continue to fear." This means that we need to have actual fear and concern as to whether our deeds will be accepted or not.

This lesson is taught in the ḥadīth where ʿĀ'isha ﵂ asked the Messenger of Allah ﷺ about the meaning of a verse of the Quran, wherein it mentions "their hearts are fearing."[34] She asked: "Are they the ones who drink and steal?" The Messenger of Allah ﷺ said, "No, O daughter of the Truthful One (*Bint al-Ṣiddīq*)! Rather, these are the ones who fast, perform prayer, and give charity, yet – despite all of this – they fear that maybe Allah will not accept their actions. These are the ones who hasten to good actions."[35]

34. Quran 23:60
35. Recorded in *Mishkāt al-Maṣābīḥ*.

This ḥadīth teaches us that our perceptions and mind-set should not be corrupted on account of doing good deeds; rather we should have fear and make *duʿā* that our deeds are accepted. We must have hope that Allah accepts, while at the same time having an ever-present fear that our deeds may not be accepted. We should nevertheless not have so much fear of them being rejected that we abandon the act of doing good deeds altogether. It is exactly for this reason that Allah ﷻ mentions, "These are the ones who hasten to do good actions."

Accordingly, the special servants of Allah ﷻ seek forgiveness even after doing good actions; whereas, the common folk only seek forgiveness for sins. The elite servants are always mindful and considering how it is even possible to ever fulfill the rights of Allah's greatness and excellence. As such, the Messenger of Allah ﷺ used to seek forgiveness thrice after every obligatory prayer. The wisdom behind this, according to the pious and righteous elders, is that the right of Allah's greatness cannot be fulfilled by anyone. For this reason, the *ʿĀrifūn* (Knowers of Allah ﷻ) seek forgiveness even after performing good deeds.

NOTE:

Someone asked the Messenger of Allah ﷺ, "A man likes that his clothing and shoes be nice. Is that arrogance?" The Messenger of Allah ﷺ said, "Allah ﷻ is Beautiful and He loves beauty. Arrogance, on the other hand, is to reject the truth and look down upon people."[36] We learn from this ḥadīth that we should not have evil thoughts of, or assume as arrogant, those pious and righteous people and Shaykhs who adorn themselves in beautiful attire. Being a pious and righteous individual or Shaykh does not mean living at the foot of a mountain, residing in a hut, eating meager bread and wearing coarse clothing; rather, it is about the condition of the heart. A person who adopts such a miserable way of life externally, but has love for the world in his heart is considered a worldly person. If, however, the love for the world is absent from one's heart, then even the king – with his vast kingdom and wealth – can be a *Walī* (friend of Allah).

اگر مال و جاه ست و زرع و تجارت

چو دل باخدا الیست خلوت نشینی

If together with wealth, honor, farming and business, one's heart is connected to Allah, Most High, at all-times;
Then he is an Allahwala[37] *and ascetic.*

This poem has been mentioned in *Maẓāhir al-Ḥaqq*, the Urdu commentary of *Mishkāt al-Maṣābīḥ*. It essentially

36. Narrated by Muslim on the authority ʿAbdullah b. Masʿūd ﷺ.
37. "Allahwala" is an Urdu term of honor that generally means, "a pious person whose focus is always on Allah". Literally, "an Allah person", or in colloquial English, a "man of God"/"man of Allah".

means that even if a person, notwithstanding his access to the above bounties, can still – at every moment – attach his heart to Allah, then he is truly an ascetic and a friend of Allah. Conversely, a person is a fraud and considered worldly if he sits at the foot of a hill or in the jungle somewhere, but is always anticipating someone bringing him gifts or sweets. In short, one can be a *faqīr* (ascetic) and Allah's friend; one can have good food, beautiful clothing, and a spacious house; one can achieve much through the companionship of pious and righteous Shaykhs; but, everything is contingent on the condition that one follows the Sunnah and is steadfast on complete piety (*taqwa*).

AN UNCERTAINTY CONCERNING ᶜ*UJUB* AND ITS ANSWER

At this point, however, an uncertainty is raised: is it considered ingratitude if Allah ﷻ grants a person some excellence in a matter, yet he does not regard it as an excellence? The answer is that we should regard it to be a quality of perfection, but should not regard it to be a product of our own excellence or achievement; instead, and more appropriately so, we should regard it to be a Divine gift and be grateful for it. Furthermore, rather than attributing that quality to ourselves – out of arrogance – we should always fear that it may be taken away from us because of some evil actions or ingratitude on our part.

DESTRUCTION OF THE SPIRITUAL WAYFARERS

Shayṭān destroys the one on the spiritual path very quickly by placing in their hearts criticism and suspicion of their Shaykh and Murabbī (one who provides spiritual nurturing).[38]

THE CURE FOR ARROGANCE

Ḥakīm al-Ummah Thānwī ؒ has prescribed several daily meditations which are highly effective in removing pride and arrogance from the heart.

Reflect upon the following:

- I have not created the excellence found within myself, rather it is a bestowal from Allah ﷻ.
- Furthermore, this gift was bestowed neither for my merit, nor for my capabilities; instead, it has been granted solely by His grace and kindness.

38. The Shaykh is one's gateway to Allah and His Messenger ﷺ. He is the fountainhead from which the student receives spiritual blessings and understanding of the path. Shayṭān tries to contaminate the source from where the Divine blessings emanate. Through this ploy, the spirituality of the student is poisoned through his objections and false suspicions, and he ends up destroying himself in the end. May Allah Most High save us all from the deceptions of the Path. Āmīn.

- Thus, to retain this bounty is also not within my control. Whenever Allah ﷻ decides to take it from me, He can take it away.

- Moreover, Allah ﷻ has the power to take away this excellence from me and grant it to the one whom I regard as a lowly person, one who does not possess this matter of excellence. Or, worse yet, Allah ﷻ can – albeit, even without taking this excellence away from me – grant him a higher level of this excellence and place him in such a lofty status that I will become dependent on him.

- Even if this person does not attain the excellence we are speaking of in the near future, there still remains the possibility that, at the present moment, Allah has granted him such an excellence that it is safely hidden from me and everyone else. Allah ﷻ is aware of this quality. Perchance it could be because of this quality that he may become more beloved and accepted than me in front of Allah.

- If the possibility of him having any excellence does not come to mind, then think that it is possible that he could be more accepted in the sight of Allah ﷻ; and, Allah ﷻ knows that the likelihood of my acceptance is

> far less, or that it is completely non-existent. Ponder, furthermore, on the Day of Judgment. Think: how many people who used to be of lowly status will be honored, and how many people who used to be of very high status will be disgraced? If this is the case, then consider what right you have to regard him as a lowly person when you do not even know of your own end result.

If contempt comes into your mind for anyone, then be good to him and treat him with kindness; make a lot of duʿā for him. Consequently, love for him will be engendered and the natural characteristic of love is that whomever one loves, one does not regard him with contempt. To further this end, ask the person how he is doing and speak to him. A relationship will likely develop on both sides and the essence of contempt will vanish.

Riyā' – Ostentation *and its Cure*

To perform good deeds with the aim of showing people and receiving praise and honor from them is referred to as showing off and ostentation. In Arabic, this is called *riyā'*. On the Day of Judgment, such noble actions, which were done for the sake of showing off, will be – instead of a means of gaining reward – a cause for punishment in the Hellfire. However, if one repents before death then there is hope of being forgiven.

Showing off manifests itself in different ways. There are times when a person shows off verbally: "Today, I have given so much charity"; or, "I am so tired because I woke up at night and performed so many units (*rakʿāt*) of *tahajjud* (night vigil prayer)"; or, "I am gifting you these prayer beads, which I brought back from my second Ḥajj." In the latter example, the reward of two Ḥajjs are ruined in one sentence.

At times, one does not utter anything verbally, but rather, shows off physically. This person may sit in front of people with his eyes closed and his head bowed – so that everyone can think that he is a very pious person and lives by the *ʿArsh* (Divine Throne), that his relationship with the *dunya* (this world) is only outwardly. But the reality is that he is engrossed in this *dunya* from head-to-toe. Other times, a person may show his eyes to be closed so that others can know that he was awake the whole night engaged in worship, and that he is being overwhelmed. Yet another form of showing off is when one lengthens the bowing and prostration in his *nawāfil* (supererogatory prayers) in people's presence – so that they may think him to be a great saint and worshipper. Summarily, all these sicknesses of showing off are created by the desire for attaining honor in the eyes of creation.

The cure for this is to ponder thus – neither will we remain, nor will creation: i.e., the ones to whom we show off our good deeds, and from whom we desire recognition and honor. All of us will eventually become dust in the graves; only the pleasure of Allah ﷻ will be of actual benefit to us. In *Mirqāt al-Mafātīḥ,* Mullā ʿAlī al-Qārī's ؒ commentary upon *Mishkāt al-Maṣābīḥ*, it is written that after Zubaydah, the wife of Hārun al-Rashīd (the caliph in Baghdad), passed away, a pious and righteous individual saw her in a dream. He asked her, "How did Allah ﷻ deal with you?" She replied, "I was forgiven." He asked, "Was it due to your work for social welfare [constructing a water canal for the pilgrims and visitants to Mecca]?" She replied, "No. All of that went to its people. Our being forgiven was due to the blessings of noble intentions." This means that when the intentions for doing social welfare work are to desire honor, fame and reputation for the works, then all of these deeds go to those false deities; these acts come to no benefit. Allah's special servants, for this reason, fear whether their works are accepted or not – despite doing good deeds. My spiritual guide, Shaykh Shāh ʿAbd al-Ghanī Phūlpūrī ؒ used to say, "Continue doing (good deeds) and fearing (whether they are accepted or not)."

This weak servant (the author), makes this *duʿā*: "O Allah! Forgive me by Your mercy; for our good actions have become mingled with show, evil, etc. because of our *nafs*."

A *duʿā* for protection from showing off has been mentioned in a noble ḥadīth. It should be read in abundance. There is hope that Allah ﷻ will protect us from this sickness through the blessing of it:

اللَّهُمَّ إِنِّي أَعُوذُ بِكَ أَنْ أُشْرِكَ بِكَ وَأَنَا أَعْلَمُ ،
وَأَسْتَغْفِرُكَ لِمَا لَا أَعْلَمُ

O Allah! I seek refuge in You from knowingly associating any partner with You, and I seek Your forgiveness for that of which I have done unknowingly.

May Allah ﷻ grant all of us sincerity!

I would like to mention one point of experience, about which all of the *Mashā'ikh* have written: The treasure of sincerity will be attained through the company and service of the friends of Allah ﷻ. Companionship of the friends of Allah ﷻ is a very important and necessary act of worship, by which the soul of sincerity is blown into all forms of worship.

THE DIFFERENCE BETWEEN *RIYĀ'*, *ʿUJUB*, & *KIBR*

Ostentation is always found in acts of worship and religious matters, while conceitedness and arrogance, on the other hand, are found in worldly and religious matters. Arrogance breeds contempt (thinking others to be lower than oneself) while conceitedness, though short of harboring contempt for others, facilitates one having an excessively favorable opinion of one's self. Conceitedness is a prerequisite for arrogance, but arrogance is not required for conceitedness.

NOTE:

If there is a person towards whom, according to the Sharīʿah, it is obligatory for you to have hatred, then do not mingle with him nor show him love. But, at the same time, you should not despise him. Have fear for your own end; it just may be possible that in the future, before his death, he may repent and go to Paradise. Mawlānā Rūmī has said:

ہیچ کافررا بخواری منگرید

کہ مسلماں بودنش باشد اُمید

Do not look at even a disbeliever with contempt;
Because it is possible that before dying,
he can become Muslim.

This means that do not even consider the Kāfir to be contemptible or lowly because he could, before dying, accept Islam. Considering him vile will only breed, in your heart, hatred for him. It is possible to have hatred in the heart for the action but not for the individual.

Let us observe, for instance, if a handsome prince has dirt smeared on his face; the dirt on his face will be detested, in so far as it is on his face, but we will not have contempt for him because we know that it is possible that he will wash his face with soap and become pure and clean again. *SubḥānAllah*! Ḥakīm al-Ummah Thānwī ☙ solved such intricate problems with examples. In short, he has said, "Hate the sin, but not the sinner: just as every one is frightened of the sickness, but still has the necessary mercy and compassion toward the patient afflicted with it."

THE DIFFERENCE BETWEEN ARROGANCE AND SHYNESS

Shyness is a natural disinclination which overtakes the *nafs* whenever we engage in an action contrary to our habit, or due to some condition that overwhelms us. The *sālik* (one treading the path to Allah ☙) may think that this disinclination is attributed to arrogance, but, in reality, it is not arrogance. The standard for measuring if it is arrogance or shyness is to ask oneself about the specific action that brings about the shame. Would you still feel the same hesitation in engaging in the action if someone honored you for it or showed you respect because of it? If the feeling is still there, then it is shyness; but if the feeling goes away, then know that it is arrogance. The interpretations of the *nafs* have to be analyzed precisely so that we do not confuse arrogance with shyness. For a detailed cure, consult your Shaykh.

ARROGANCE IN THE FORM OF HUMILITY

Ḥakīm al-Ummah Thānwī ؒ said, "At times, arrogance comes in the form of humility." This means that, at times, a person displays humility so that people will regard him as being great. The sign of this is that after being humble, if people do not honor and respect him, he feels bad. A true *Allahwala*[39] does not regard himself worthy of respect.

JEALOUSY

Jealousy is when one feels displeased with the favorable conditions or bounties of another person, and further desires those bounties to be taken away from that person. This sickness is extremely dangerous. It has the propensity to not only rob one of peace and tranquility, but to also set the heart on fire. The ḥadīth mentions, "Jealousy consumes the good

---

39. See previous footnote.

actions of the jealous person just as fire consumes wood."[40] Mawlānā Shāh Muḥammad Aḥmad Ṣāḥib ﷺ has beautifully composed two poems on jealousy:

حسد کی آگ میں کیوں جل رہے ہو
کفِ افسوس تم کیوں مل رہے ہو
خدا کے فیصلے سے کیوں ہو ناراض
جہنم کی طرف کیوں چل رہے ہو

Why are you burning in the flame of jealousy?
Why are you rubbing your hands in sorrow?
Why are you upset with Allah's decision?
Why are you moving toward Jahannam?

Ḥakīm al-Ummah Thānwī ﷺ has said, "If your heart rejoices at the misfortune of either a friend or foe – even though you show sorrow outwardly, then known that this is sign of imperfection. This is still the case even though inner happiness is non-volitional and not considered a sin. Cure this forcefully by invoking numerous *duʿās* for that person. Allah willing, abundant *duʿā* will remove this imperfection."

40. Narrated by Abū Dāwūd and Ibn Mājah on the authority of Abū Hurayrah ﷺ

THE CURE FOR JEALOUSY

To cure jealousy do the following:

- Precede him in giving salutations of peace (saying, "*al-salām ʿalaykum*").
- Meet him before going on a journey.
- Upon returning from a journey, bring him a gift, even if it is small in value.
- Praise him in your gatherings.
- Occasionally invite him for a meal.
- Make abundant *duʿā* for him.
- Censure anyone who speaks ill of him and let the person know that it is *ḥarām* (unlawful) to backbite as well as to listen to it.

Allah willing, a few days of practicing these guidelines will cure this sickness. Subsequently, instead of brooding and burning within due to jealousy, you will attain love for the person and your heart will be alleviated and enlivened like the magnificent rose. It will become tranquil and unfettered, ready for the remembrance and worship of Allah ﷻ.

MALICE AND ITS CURE

If a person suffers harm, but does not have the ability to avenge himself, then a slight amount of anger remains in the heart. If by controlling this anger, a burden is felt his heart and he begins to desire evil for his antagonist, then this is called malice. Sometimes this malice can reach harmful proportions and lead to many other evils such as violence, jealousy, anger, hatred, harboring a grudge, stress and anxiety. This malice, however, is cured by forgiving the antagonist and forcing oneself to mingle with him. Besides this, the remaining aspects of the cure are the same as has been mentioned above regarding jealousy.

THE CURE FOR GREED AND LOVE OF THE WORLD

The best cure for greed and love of this world is to attend the gatherings of the friends of Allah ﷻ and to learn from them the manner of acquiring a relationship with Allah. The heart will automatically become disinclined from this world as one's connection with Allah ﷻ becomes more deeply rooted. Only through the remembrance of Allah ﷻ and with the company of the friends of Allah can the sickness of greed and love of this world be removed.

Additionally, it is also very beneficial to ponder abundantly on the uncertainty of this world, and to give thought to death. Reciting these poems in abundance will also purify the heart from the love of this world:

دبا کے قبر میں سب چل دیے دعا نہ سلام

ذرا سی دیر میں کیا ہو گیا زمانے کو

After burying me in the grave, they all have left;
Without duʿā, without salām;
What has happened to people in such a short while?

یہ چمن صحرا بھی ہوگا یہ خبر بلبل کو دو

تاکہ اپنی زندگی کو سوچ کے قرباں کرے

Inform the nightingale that this garden
will one day become a desert;
So that it may ponder before sacrificing its life.

آکر قضا باہوش کو بے ہوش کر گئی

ہنگامۂ حیات کو خاموش کر گئی

Death came and rendered the conscious unconscious;
It simply silenced the activities of life.

قضا کے سامنے بے کار ہوتے ہیں حواس اکبر
کُھلی ہوتی ہیں گو آنکھیں مگر بینا نہیں ہوتیں

In front of death, the senses become useless, O Akbar;
The eyes are open but they are unable to see.

قضا کے بعد ہوئی سرد نفس کی دنیا
نہ حُسن و عشق کے جھگڑے نہ مال و دولت کے

After death came, rendered cold and lifeless
was the world of the nafs
Gone were the squabbles, of beauty and love,
of property and wealth

Visit the graveyard from time to time and witness with your own eyes the final result and condition of the worldly people. Where are their luxurious homes, their vehicles, their wealth, and their servants? Now only their good deeds can assist them.

شکریہ اے قبر تک پہنچانے والوں شکریہ
اب اکیلے ہی چلے جائیں گے اس منزل سے ہم

Thanks, to you who is conveying
my body to the grave, thanks;
Now I will be going all alone from this stage onward.

Just as one prisoner does not have the requisite authority to grant freedom to another prisoner – that freedom must come from qualified individuals from outside of the prison, so too is the worldly person unable to free another worldly person from the love and fetters of this world. The liberation from the love of this world will require being in the company of the people of Allah who are in the world physically, but that their souls have transcended it. The following is a poem of mine:

دنیا کے مشغلوں میں بھی یہ باخدا رہے
یہ سب کے ساتھ رہ کے بھی سب سے جدا رہے

Even in the pre-occupation of the world,
he remained devoted to Allah, Most Exalted;
Being with all, he remained isolated from all.

Inappropriate Anger and its Cure

During anger, the intellect does not remain sound and the angry person is rendered unable to think about the consequences of his actions. Accordingly, the tongue begins expressing unfitting and inappropriate words while excessive and oppressive acts are committed by the hands. Sometimes a person inflamed by anger will even pronounce three divorces on his wife, resulting in a lifetime of sorrow and remorse. The impulsiveness of anger can even force one to strike others without thinking, without restraint; to even go as far as taking human life, whereby destroying homes and families, extinguishing their light for generations on end. A ḥadīth states, "Anger is from Shayṭān, and Shayṭān has been created from fire. The cure for fire is water. Thus, when anger comes, make *wuḍū'*."[41]

The cure for anger is that one should get away from the person who has angered him. If the person who has angered you does not go away on his own accord, then you should see to it that you get away from him forthwith. Subsequently, you should call to mind the fact that even though this person has wronged you, taken your right and disobeyed you, that we – even still – commit more acts of injustice and disobedience day and night because we continue to disobey Allah ﷻ on a much greater scale and are ever more negligent in fulfilling His rights. Despite this, Allah ﷻ does not take away His bounties from us, nor His favors that He has bestowed upon us.

We should take into account that just as we desire that Allah ﷻ should forgive our sins, then, similarly, we should desire to forgive the sins of Allah's servants. Our desire for forgiving Allah's servants and bestowing favors upon them should be equal to the degree of forgiveness we desire for

41. Narrated by Aḥmad in his *Musnad* on the authority of ʿAṭiyyah al-ʿAwfī ؓ

ourselves on the Day of Judgment. Reminding yourself of this will ultimately begin to, Allah willing, assuage your heart.

In addition to this, recite *aʿūdhu billāhi minash Shayṭānir rajīm* (I seek refuge in Allah from the Rejected Shayṭān) a few times; make *wuḍū'* and drink cold water; sit down, if you are standing; lie down, if you are sitting; and remind yourself of Allah's anger. Once your anger lessens and your mind is restored to a sound state, then commence to selecting an appropriate remedy for the situation. An example of this would be as follows: if for the purpose of disciplining of your children you have to exhibit anger, then only after your anger subsides and you have carefully deliberated on the consequences should you reprimand, and solely according to the allowable limits of the *Sharīʿah*. By repeating this method, anger will be reformed.

Controlling one's anger feels like a burden on the *nafs*, but its outcome is always favorable; by virtue of this control, even the enemy becomes a friend. But giving in to anger, on the other hand, renders one's friend a foe. Moreover, due to his evil character on account of anger, one is, slowly and constantly, deprived of all allies and left abandoned.

There is the example of one such person who was extremely evil-natured and prone to – because of his ill-temperament – abusing his neighbors. When his wife passed away, he was forced to hire workers to carry the Janaza (i.e., no one wanted to volunteer to aid him). Allah's Messenger "A strong person is not one who defeats others in wrestling; a strong person is one who controls himself at the time of anger."[42]

Allah ﷻ has praised those who swallow their anger, those who forgive the wrong-doings of people, and those who treat people with excellence. In addition to that, one should think that everything occurs by the command of Allah ﷻ. For example, if someone suffers loss to his wealth,[43] then he should know that only through the exercise of patience will he receive the due reward. Furthermore, by reciting the phrase *innā lillāhi wa innā ilayhi rājiʿūn* (Verily we are from Allah and to Him is our return), one is promised an even better bounty in return. Conversely, one should think that by taking revenge, not only is the reward lost, but that one loses all opportunity to attain benefit from the matter. Worse yet, if anger provokes one to take revenge and subsequently oppress the other party, then one will also have to bear Allah's punishment and seizure.

EXEMPLARY INCIDENTS OF CONTROLLING ANGER

THE FIRST INCIDENT

A pious and righteous Shaykh, Abū Yazīd al-Bisṭāmī ؒ, was walking along when an enemy of his threw a basket of

42. Narrated by al-Bukhārī and Muslim on the authority of Abū Hurayrah ؓ.
43. This section refers to the desire for revenge that may arise in the specific instances of financial crimes, such as theft, fraud, etc.

ashes on top of his head. Abū Yazīd said, "*Alḥamdulillāh* (All praise is due to Allah)!" His disciples asked, "Was this an occasion to say *Alḥamdulillāh*?" He replied, "For the one who was worthy of being burnt by fire due to his sins, why should he not be grateful that only ashes fell on him?"

THE SECOND INCIDENT

Two men were fighting in front of Mawlānā Rūmī ﵀. One man said to the other, "If you curse me once, I will curse you ten times." Mawlānā Rūmī said, "Curse at me one thousand times, I will not reply with even one vulgar word." Both of them fell down, kissed his feet, and reconciled.

THE THIRD INCIDENT:

Shaykh al-Ḥadīth, Mawlānā Muḥammad Zakariyyah ﵀ rebuked a servant, who then sought forgiveness. The Shaykh said, "You're always troubling me like this. How long do I have to tolerate this attitude from you?" His uncle, Mawlānā Ilyās Ṣāḥib ﵀, was sitting close by. He whispered into his ear, "Mawlānā, as much as you want Allah ﷻ to tolerate you in the Hereafter, then you should, to that extent, tolerate His servants in this life." This means that we should forgive the shortcomings of people in this world according to the level of forgiveness that we would like to see from Allah for our shortcomings in the next world.

A BEAUTIFUL AND EFFECTIVE REFLECTION TO CURE ANGER

When anger completely overcomes you, immediately think, "If I, at this time, control my anger over this person and forgive him, then Allah ﷻ, on the Day of Judgment, will hold back His punishment from me." This glad tiding is found in the narration of Anas b. Mālik ؓ.

EVIL GLANCES, TREACHERY OF THE HEART, AND WORSHIPING OF BEAUTY

Among all the evil character traits, this sickness is considered extremely dangerous. In the beginning, its harms are not perceived. A person initially thinks; "I am looking at these beauties merely for enjoyment; I'm not giving or taking anything." This thought is a mere deception because through evil glances and filthy thoughts, not only is the heart affected, but also sexual passions are aroused. Subsequently, the health begins to deteriorate and the enjoyment of worship is quickly sapped away. He will not experience any joy in *dhikr* and worship. Some conditions even lead to disastrous results. May Allah ﷻ save us!

Due to one person's evil glances, the love of a beautiful woman penetrated his heart to such an extent that even when he was told to repent, he said, "I repent from all sins; however, I will not repent from the extreme love I have for my beloved!" When he was told to recite the *kalimah*,[44] he replied, "The pleasure of my lover is more beloved and valuable to me than the mercy of Allah!" (May Allah ﷻ protect us!) Death found him in this state of disbelief.

Shayṭān makes a determined effort to involve spiritual wayfarers in these two sicknesses: the trap of women and the love of handsome boys.

NOTE:

At times, Shayṭān affects a person's gaze, effectively mesmerizing him to the extent that even an ordinary looking person appears extremely handsome to him. In every gaze, there are – hidden from sight – thousands of arrows from the quivers of Shayṭān. Mawlānā Rūmī ؒ has referred to this condition as *tamwīh* (distortion, deception). This is a very dangerous condition. Ḥakīm al-Ummah Thānwī ؒ has mentioned of this state, "O Allah! Protect Ashraf ʿAlī from this condition!" He further writes, "When Allah ﷻ, through His mercy, saves one from this condition, then this condition is called *tambīh* (awakening)."

It is astonishing that some foolish people do not regard these things as sins. They carry in one hand some prayer beads while staring at women and young boys with an evil

44. The statement "Lā ilāha illā Allah" (There is no god but Allah)

intent, though the *Sharīʿah* has made *ḥarām* (unlawful) both of these actions and considers them dangerous sins. The one who persists and continuously perpetrates these actions is a transgressor and an open sinner. Such a person will not even attain a whiff of the fragrance of Allah's closeness.

Worshipping of beauty and evil glances destroy physical as well as spiritual health. They cause one to become disgraced in this life and in the Hereafter. If one is afflicted with this sickness during his student days, then his heart mind, and memory will be weakened; plus, it will eliminate knowledge from his heart. This sickness deprives the seeker of religious knowledge – from the blessings of that knowledge and piety. It leaves him eternally bereft of perfection and progress in knowledge and action.

One should, therefore, treat this sickness with great concern, care, and determination. Never regard this poison as honey and never regard this cause of destruction as a cause of happiness and joy. When Allah ﷻ has commanded us to protect our gazes, how can there be any benefit or goodness in this action? Who can be more well-wishing for His servants than Allah ﷻ? In short, evil glances and worshipping of beauty are extremely dangerous sicknesses which destroy one's religious and worldly life. There is not sufficient space in this booklet for lengthy details concerning this, but if you want to study their harms in more detail, refer to this weak servant's book, *Remedies for Spiritual Maladies*.

THE CURE FOR EVIL GLANCES AND WORSHIPING OF BEAUTY

This sickness afflicts on different levels, according to people's respective natures. Some suffer from it severely, while others suffer to an even greater extent. Some people even succumb to this illness as soon as they attain maturity.

REFORMATION FOR CHILDREN

This is an extremely important chapter for parents to take into consideration, especially due to fact that we are surrounded by shamelessness and immodesty in the form of internet pornography and its various manifestations on social media. Early intervention will help our children protect themselves from the evils and ill effects of these destructive sins that have the effect of destroying our *iman*.

Parents should, even from early childhood, be concerned about saving their children from this illness. If a person destroys his youth, he will inevitably be deprived of attaining academic excellence. Keep a careful watch over your children from a young age. Keep them far away from unsupervised internet usage, television, and evil company. In addition to this, instill in them the fear of Allah and the punishment of the Hellfire. Take them to the gatherings of pious and righteous

Shaykhs from time to time. As much as possible, do not keep your children away from your care. While they are young, do not leave them and journey out of the country, unless there is a dire need to do so. In the absence of the father, children quickly become audacious and uninhibited. Often because the mother cannot control them, they can become careless as a result. Continue making fervent *duʿā* to Allah ﷻ for the piety of your children. Read this *duʿā* after every obligatory prayer:

رَبَّنَا هَبْ لَنَا مِنْ أَزْوٰجِنَا وَذُرِّيّٰتِنَا قُرَّةَ أَعْيُنٍ،
وَاجْعَلْنَا لِلْمُتَّقِينَ إِمَامًا

O our Lord! Make our spouses and our
offspring a coolness for our eyes,
and make us the leaders of the righteous people.

Keep your children engaged in different positive and permissible activities. By having a busy life, one is generally protected from Shayṭānic traps.

REFORMATION FOR THOSE WHO ARE MATURE

THE FIRST STEP

Make a habit of doing some *dhikr* daily. If there is any pious and righteous Shaykh in your locality, consult with him.

Otherwise, recite salutations upon the Prophet three hundred times, *Lā ilāha illā Allah* one hundred times, and invoke "*Allah, Allah*" one hundred times. Recite a portion of Quran daily and be punctual in offering the *ishrāq*[45], *awwābīn*[46], and *tahajjud*[47] prayers. If you are unable to awaken in the last portion of the night, then perform two or four *rakaʿāt* of *nafl* (supererogatory prayer) after performing the *Sunnah* of the *ʿIshā'* prayer; but, before the *witr*, with the intention of *tahajjud*. By having punctuality in *dhikr*, recitation, and optional prayers, light will be created in the heart. The light of Truth (Allah ﷻ) cools the fire of desires. Mawlānā Rūmī ؓ said, "The fire of the sensual desires of the *nafs* can only be cooled by the light of Allah ﷻ."

NOTE:

One important point to remember is that some people obey the demands of sin, desiring, thereby, to weaken it. They feel that by committing the sin, the desire and demand of sin will lessen. This is a clear deception, however. With every sin, the desire to commit more sins only increases. There is only a temporary, momentary decrease; but, immediately thereafter, the flame rises even more than before. The thought

45. A nafl (supererogatory) prayer of two or four rakaʿāt that is offered after the sun has fully risen in the morning.

46. A *nafl* prayer of six *rakaʿ*āt that is offered after the *Maghrib* prayer.

47. A *nafl* prayer that is offered in the latest part of the night, prior to the entering of *Fajr*.

of lessening sin by sin is like one who washes feces with urine, thinking that the impurity of the feces will be lessened. People engaged in this thinking always remain perplexed and will never become pure from sin. Therefore, muster the courage to not obey the demands of sin. If, however, from time to time, one is overpowered and he misuses his eyes, then he should perform at least four *rakʿāt* of *nafl*, give some charity, and repent sincerely and remorsefully.

When the desire to sin arises, you need to muster courage. Make *duʿā* intensely. Perform two *rakaʿāt* of *ṣalāt al-Ḥājah*[48] and seek Allah's protection. Engage yourself in some permissible and good work, visit a friend to enliven yourself, and involve yourself in running errands or other necessities for your wife and children. Consequently, the inclination and intensity of the thoughts of the *nafs* will be weakened. Soon, it will be overpowered and non-existent. This prescription is very beneficial. Khawāja Ṣāḥib ﷺ composed it in poetic form. These are all the advices of Ḥakīm al-Ummah Thānwī ﷺ:

طبیعت کی روزور پر ہے تو رُک
نہیں تو یہ سر سے گزر جائے گی

ذرا دیر کو تُو ہٹالے خیال
چڑھی ہے یہ ندی اُتر جائے گی

48. A nafl prayer that is offered when there is some necessity that needs to be fulfilled.

When the desire (to sin) is strong, then stop it;
If not, it will pass over your head.
For a short while, remove thoughts of it;
This river which has risen will descend.

Do not be afraid to strive in this manner; be prepared to control this sorrow your whole life. This is what being an ʿāshiq (ardent lover) is all about: that you place the neck of every desire of your *nafs* under the sword of Allah's command, that you should happily bear whatever difficulty may come in restraining yourself from sin or in protecting your eyes. This is a martyr fighting in *al-jihād al-akbar* (the greatest Jihad). Even though he is alive, internally he is constantly being martyred.

ترے حکم کی تیغ سے میں ہوں بسمل
شہادت نہیں میری ممنونِ خنجر

I am being slaughtered by the sword of
Your commandment;
My martyrdom is not indebted to a dagger

Becoming a martyr under the sword of a disbeliever is easy; it happens once. In this great *jihād*, however, one is forced to wave the sword of the Divine commands over his evil desires for the duration of his whole life.

کمالِ عشق تو مر مر کے جینا ہے نہ مر جانا
ابھی اس راز سے واقف نہیں ہیں ہائے پروانے

Perfection of love is not to die, but to live dying
(breaking your desires);
O the moth[49] *is not as yet aware of this secret.*

SECOND STEP

One should remain under the supervision of a friend of Allah ﷻ for a complete cure. Until the spiritually sick person attains, in the heart, a special connection with Allah ﷻ – referred to as *nisbah bāṭiniyyah* – he must remain in the company of a completed guide: a guide who follows the *Sunnah,* has piety, and has been authorized by his guide before him to instruct those striving on the spiritual path. Thus, by attaining this connection with Allah ﷻ, it becomes much easier for a spiritual wayfarer to protect his *nafs*.

Ḥakīm al-Ummah Thānwī ؒ has given a prescription for saving oneself from all sins in just two lines: [1] Before sinning, prevent your *nafs* with all your might. [2] If you err due to the evil of your *nafs*, repent with a sincere heart.

Continue beseeching for protection in the Divine court by making *duʿā* earnestly and humbly. Likewise, keep the place of your prostration wet with tears. If, for some reason, you are unable to cry, then at least imitate the form of a crying

49. Refers to the lover

person. This is because *duʿā* is a great bounty and a means of attaining Allah's mercy and grace. Furthermore, only by the grace of Allah ﷻ can a servant be both protected from sins and also capable of fulfilling the Divine commands.

Mawlānā Rūmī ؒ once said, "O Allah! Even if thousands of traps of sins are in front of us, if Your grace is with us, to assist us, then we have no worries!" He also said, "By not having the kindness and grace of Allah ﷻ, the one hunting the deer becomes entrapped in the jaws of the boar."

Therefore, you can never be proud of your piety and abstinence; rather, be afraid at all times. Continue making *duʿā* and crying to Allah ﷻ for protection. Never acknowledge your own strength, instead regard your success to be based on humility. Even the pious person – as firm as an elephant or a lion – will, undoubtedly, slip and suffer destruction if Allah ﷻ were to remove His grace, kindness, and assistance from him. But, on the other hand, if Allah ﷻ manifests His grace and kindness – as our protector and consoler – then even the spiritual wayfarer who is as weak as a mosquito will be honored and bestowed with the highest stages of Divine closeness. You will see the schemes and plots of Shayṭān and *nafs* running away from the lion-like courage of this man; you will see them fleeing just as the deer, cheetahs, stags, and many other large horned animals run away from the lion.

Also in this sickness, Shayṭān has the propensity to attack a person and make him feel despondent. When a spiritual wayfarer, after spending a period of time in *dhikr* and contemplation, and after spending time in the company of the friends of Allah ﷻ, still perceives within himself the evil demands of his *nafs*, he – unfortunately – becomes despondent and begins to think, "I cannot remain on this path." Be that as it may, it is people like this who need to stay on the path. This path is not for the faint of heart; it is the path of those who possess strong will and determination.

Know that piety (*taqwa*) is defined as restraint from acting upon desires – the dictates of sin. Hence, were it not for these desires, how would piety even come into existence? Therefore, do not become fearful of having to strive and make effort your entire life; the struggle gradually becomes easier. But, on the other hand, if your desires become strong and lead to agitation because you did not abstain from evil glances, then know that it is your own fault. The path in and of itself was never difficult; you made it difficult. In any case, do not lose courage, regardless of the condition you are in. Khawāja Ṣāḥib ؒ has beautifully stated:

نہ چت کر سکے نفس کے پہلواں کو
تو یوں ہاتھ پاؤں بھی ڈھیلے نہ ڈالے
ارے اس سے کشتی تو ہے عمر بھر کی
کبھی وہ دبا لے کبھی تُو دبا لے

If you cannot defeat the wrestler of the nafs;
Then do not leave your hands and feet loose.
You have to fight it your whole life;
Sometimes it succeeds and sometimes you succeed.

Sometimes, Shayṭān makes people lose hope and says: "What reward and Divine closeness will a person like you ever attain; someone who has broken his repentance over and over again? Such unworthy people like you will remain deprived of His high court. This is the path of pious people." The answer to this is that – undoubtedly – the breaking of our repentance is a grave sin, but that we do not have any other refuge; essentially, we have no other God to turn to besides Him. No matter where we go, there is no other place for us besides Allah ﷻ. And, if He is only a *Rabb* (Creator, Sustainer, and Lord) for the pious, then is there another *Rabb* for us sinners, to whom we can turn? We are also His creation. We will repent and cry before Him, making Him pleased.

Ḥakīm al-Ummah Thānwī ﵀ said, "If the one who repents is not raised up with the perfect ones, he will definitely be raised with the penitent, Allah willing." A noble ḥadīth says, "O Allah, nothing can hold back Your favors." In that case, why should one become despondent? Instead, continue beseeching Allah ﷻ for His mercy because whatever you receive, it will only come to you by Allah's grace.

This advice is being offered, therefore, only to save you from despondency, not to embolden you to commit sin. Fear disobeying Allah ﷻ just as you fear a snake or scorpion. Continuously make sincere *duʿā* for your own reformation and ask your friends and elders to make *duʿā* also. Moreover, ask your spiritual guide and Shayk – continuously make requests to him for *duʿā*.

بس ہے اپنا ایک نالہ بھی اگر پہنچے وہاں
گرچہ کرتے ہیں بہت سے نالہ و فریاد ہم

It is sufficient for just one lamentation
of ours to reach there (to Allah);
Even though we engage in many
lamentations and appeals.

This poetic couplet means that the day that one request – one *duʿā* – is accepted, our work will be done. Although, it goes without saying that every *duʿā* and cry of ours reaches there (to Allah). In this poem, however, reaching means acceptance.

The most effective and successful cure is to establish a connection with a qualified spiritual guide. Inform him of all the conditions relating to your reformation. Whatever he proposes, act upon it with your heart and soul.

EVIL THOUGHTS AND THEIR CURE

By this illness, other illnesses of enmity, hatred, disdain of others, jealousy, and backbiting are created. When an evil thought occurs regarding someone, immediately think, "I will have to present evidence on the Day of Judgment for this evil thought. I do not possess any definitive evidence, so why should I fall into this dispute? Why don't I have good thoughts so that I can continue receiving reward without evidence?"

The one who carries tales from one place to another, creating enmity and hatred among the Muslims, is referred to as a talebearer. The cure for such a person is to seize him by the hand and take him to the person who he is gossiping about. Ask that person, "This person is narrating this speech of yours to me, saying that you have backbitten me." If it turns out to be false, then he will never carry tales again. If, however, it is proved true, then the person who has backbitten you will feel ashamed and seek pardon. That person will never again possess the courage to backbite you again.

TWENTY EVILS OF THE TONGUE

1. To engage in futile speech.
2. To speak more than is necessary.

3. To needlessly narrate tales of sinners and wrongdoers.
4. To unnecessarily argue and debate.
5. To fight and quarrel.
6. To exaggerate and embellish.
7. To be profane (to curse).
8. To be foul-mouthed and to utter disrespectful words to elders.
9. To invoke *laʿnāt* (curses).
10. To sing songs and poems contrary to the *Sharīʿah*.
11. To laugh excessively.
12. To speak to someone in a belittling manner.
13. To expose someone's secret.
14. To make false promises.
15. To speak lies. However, if one lies to make peace between two Muslims, or if an oppressed person speaks a lie so that he can receive his right, then this is permissible.
16. To backbite. This means to speak in someone's absence such words that if he was present he would feel bad, even if it is true. This action is forbidden.

The good deeds of those who backbite will be taken away and given to the other person.

17. To carry tales.
18. To praise or flatter someone in his presence. However, if there is no fear of pride entering his heart by your praises (rather his spirits will be raised to do good actions), then there is no harm.
19. To be unconcerned with subtle (but grievous) errors in one's speech. Some people say, "Shaykh, whatever *duʿā* emerges from your mouth will definitely be accepted" or "Above Allah is our support and below, is yours." All such speech is *shirk* (polytheism).
20. For the general public to ask scholars questions which have no relevance or connection to their necessities. It is a waste of their time to ask futile and unnecessary questions.

The Cure for the Diseases of the Tongue

The cure for all the ailments of the tongue is that one should always think before speaking, "Whatever I want to say, will my Master and Sustainer be happy with it or not?" If the thought comes that He will be happy, then speak; on the contrary, if there is fear that He will be displeased, then remain silent. Shaykh Saʿdī ﷺ said, "Do not speak without thinking, even if you have to remain silent for a while. How can there be sorrow in silence which is then followed up with words that yield benefit?"

AN INCIDENT:

After an extended period of drought, heavy rain suddenly came. Upon seeing this, a pious and righteous individual exclaimed, "Splendid! Today, Allah, Most Exalted, has sent down the rain at the right time!" An inspiration came to him forthwith, "O disrespectful one! Did We ever send down rain at the wrong time?" He immediately began weeping and repented with great regret. Hence, one should be very cautious in his speech.

BACKBITING

This refers to speaking ill of a Muslim in his absence, or of relating anything negative about him – such as about his children, vehicle, or house – to others. This could be done verbally or by hand gestures: e.g., making a sign that he is short; pointing to one's eye to indicate that he is blind or blind in one eye; bending one's back to allude that someone has a bent back; or, raising one leg and walking to indicate towards someone's limp. In essence, this refers to mentioning your brother in such a way that if he were present, then he would most assuredly be saddened or upset by the expressions, even if they were true. Thus, when you speak about any person, first think that if he were present, would he be pleased or displeased with your speech or gestures? If your heart feels that he would be displeased, then this is backbiting; and it is backbiting even if what is being said or expressed is true. If, on the other hand, what is being expressed is not even ztrue, then it is referred to as *buhtān* (slander); and this, obviously, is prohibited.

Some people, taking advantage of their connection or relationship with an individual, will make mention of the person's house, vehicle, wife, or children in such a way that if he were present, he would have felt bad about it. This is also considered backbiting. Nevertheless, if, with the intention of reformation, one informs parents of their children, teachers of their students, or spiritual guides of their *murīds*, then it is not considered backbiting. Similarly, if you are made aware of someone intending to cause harm to somebody else, then to inform the potential victim with the intention of saving him from harm is obligatory. Furthermore, this encompasses having concern for your Muslim brother.

A ḥadīth states that backbiting is more grievous than fornication. Scholars have stated that the reason for this is that fornication is a violation of Allah's rights; hence, if one desires forgiveness and repentance from Allah ﷻ then there is always hope of being forgiven. However, backbiting is a violation of a servant's right. This means that as long as the person does not forgive, then the guilty party will not be granted forgiveness.

Ḥakīm al-Ummah Thānwī ﷺ said, "Backbiting is both the father and son of enmity." That is to say that backbiting, more often than not, gives birth to enmity and hatred; and, at other times, the underlying enmity that already exists gives birth to the backbiting that ensues. As a result, we can understand how despicable a sin this can be, how evil a lineage it could bear, where it acts as both the father and the son.

Nowadays, there is hardly any gathering in which backbiting is not found. Never mind the general masses, even the scholars and the elite are involved in it. Ḥakīm al-Ummah Thānwī ﷺ has, for this reason, encouraged the abandonment of this sin with extra emphasis.

If you have been granted the ability to do so, then seek forgiveness from those you have backbitten. However, if the person is unaware of your backbiting and, if, by seeking forgiveness and informing him, there is a fear of causing sorrow and creating hatred and enmity in the heart, then instead just make a firm and sincere intention that you will not backbite him in the future. In addition to this, you should praise the victim of the backbiting, especially in the company of those among whom he had been backbitten; acknowledge the mistake of backbiting; and, finally, make *duʿā* for him. Furthermore, Quran should be recited (at least *Sūrah al-Ikhlāṣ* three times a day, if not more) for some time afterwards and the rewards of it conveyed to the one who was backbitten. There is hope that on the Day of Judgment, Allah ﷻ will ask those people who had been backbitten to forgive this sin. It is hoped that when these people see for themselves the rewards that were sent to them, then they will feel mercy and forgive those who transgressed against them.

Needless to say, just because *iṣāl al-thawāb* (the conveyance of reward) makes up for the sin of backbiting, one should not use it as an excuse or a dispensation to then engage in backbiting; Allah ﷻ is well aware of our intention within our hearts. There is also the added fear that one could secure an evil end for himself by backbiting someone who is considered an accepted servant of Allah ﷻ. Moreover, no one can discern who is accepted by Allah ﷻ and who is not because a person may outwardly appear to be a simple, ordinary Muslim, while – all along – some of his deeds done in solitude may have caused him to achieve a high and noble status in the sight of Allah ﷻ.

Similarly, the opposite also holds true. On the Day of Judgment, how many people, who used to be of very high status, will be disgraced; and, how many people who used to be of lowly status will be honored? May Allah ﷻ grant us all the ability to honor all Muslims and abstain from backbiting. *Āmīn*!

The usual causes of backbiting are evil thoughts and arrogance. But, if one is more concerned about his own condition, then his gaze will not fall onto the faults of others. Ḥakīm al-Ummah Thānwī ﵀ said, "Whoever has concern for his own evil condition, he will at all times fear Allah Most Exalted with regard to himself so much that – never mind fellow Muslims – he will see himself as worse than disbelievers and, worse yet, even animals."

Ḥaḍrat Saʿdī Shīrāzī ﵀ said:

They became as honorable as the angels,
Because they considered themselves
lower than the animals...

The friends of Allah ﷻ, because of the fear that they hold as to their eventual outcome on the plains of Resurrection, do not even regard themselves better than, say, dogs. The reason for this is that dogs, and even pigs, for that matter, are better than a person who meets an evil end because there is no punishment in Hell for these animals. The friends of Allah ﷻ on the other hand, can – due to the degree of their servitude and self-annihilation – even surpass the angels in terms of honor. This is because Allah ﷻ, more than anything else, desires humility, servitude and self-annihilation from His servants. Likewise, it is not strength that will avail anyone on the Day of Judgment; rather, only by crying and humbling oneself before Allah ﷻ, will one attain the objective. This is the essence not only of *sulūk* (spiritual wayfaring) and *taṣawwuf* (sufism), but of humanity itself.

In fact, whoever possesses such humility will show compassion to all of creation: he will neither cause harm to anyone, nor take revenge. The erudite scholar Abū 'l-Qāsim al-Qushayrī ؒ has written, "A person who takes revenge, becoming overpowered by the fervor of revenge, can never be a friend of Allah ﷻ. A friend of Allah ﷻ is one who is forbearing and who continues making *duʿā* for those who vex and trouble him." Mawlānā Shāh Muḥammad Aḥmad Ṣāḥib ؒ has composed this amazing couplet:

جور و ستم سے جس نے کیا دل کو پاش پاش
احمد نے اس کو بہی تہہ دل سے دعا دیا

Whoever has broken my heart
into bits by his oppression;
Aḥmad has also made duʿā for him
from the depths of his heart.

Some people are quite advanced and particular in praying *ishrāq* and *awwābīn* and performing *dhikr*, *murāqabah* (meditation) and *tasbiḥāt*; however, as soon as someone causes them any difficulty, or when something happens contrary to their temperament, they immediately place their prayer beads in their pockets and resort to uttering obscenities and using vulgar language. They do not discern whom they are addressing – whether it is someone older or younger, whether it is their parents, teacher, or Shaykh. No – they, at that point, forget everything. It is regarding such people that this statement is most known:

"At one moment they are saints,
at another they are beasts."

Whoever keeps the anger of Allah ﷻ before himself at all times (i.e., is continuously reflecting on it) will forget his own anger. One's own anger can be used, however, but only in the pleasure of Allah ﷻ and after the *nafs* has been thoroughly annihilated. Consider the fact that before accepting Islam, ʿUmar's ؓ anger was used against Muslims; but, through the nurturing of the Messenger of Allah ﷺ and because of the blessings of his company, this same anger was then reversed and used against the disbelievers and hypocrites. Similarly, if a person's anger is reformed, he will use his anger against his own *nafs,* to abstain from sin; he will forgive the errors of Allah's creation so as to gain forgiveness from Allah; he will show compassion and mercy to them; and, finally, he will compel his *nafs* to respect elders, have compassion with the young, and honor the scholars. Although this may seem difficult in the beginning, practicing this for a period of time, nonetheless, will eventually make it into a habit and a natural disposition.

Ḥakīm al-Ummah Thānwī ﷺ said, "You will not see a person about to be hanged backbiting a person caught for a minor crime, nor will you see a person suffering from leprosy laughing at one who has a minor cough." Therefore, the one whose gaze is fixed on the terrifying reckoning and the final outcome on the Day of Judgment will neither laugh at nor backbite others; he will neither have the time nor courage to do so. My poem is:

نا مناسب ہے اے دلِ ناداں
اِک جذامی ہنسے زکامی پر

Truly inappropriate it is, O foolish heart;
For one suffering leprosy to laugh
at one with a common cold!

LYING

The Messenger of Allah ﷺ said, "Hold firmly to the truth. Verily truthfulness guides a person to good deeds, which leads him to Paradise. And, abstain from lying. Lying leads a person to wrong-doing, which leads him to Hell."[50]

NOTE:

Some people tell lies just to make others laugh. These people are actually using the laughter of others as a means to secure their own sorrow on the Day of Judgment

VULGAR LANGUAGE

There are times when even the learned people and those engaged in *dhikr*, meditation, and worship succumb to anger and end up using vulgarity in their speech. Vulgarity in speech, however, is always contrary to self-honor, shame, and dignity. One should ponder, instead: "How can we utter such impure words with the same mouth with which we recite the Holy Quran, send salutations upon the Prophet ﷺ, and take the pure name of Allah ﷻ?" It is for this reason that the pious and honorable people were not known for using vulgarity in speech.

This sickness generally occurs when a person is consumed by anger; therefore, the cure for it is the same as that for anger, namely: utilize your courage and determination, save yourself from disgrace and embarrassment, reflect upon the Divine act of Allah's listening – i.e., that Allah ﷻ is listening

50. Muslim

to your foolish utterances. Also, if you have exhibited anger towards anyone unjustly, cursed at him, or used vulgar language with him, then take advantage of the opportunity to humble yourself before him and seek his forgiveness, no matter how much your *nafs* feels disgraced in doing so. Reflect upon the fact that the difficulty here is much less than the difficulty of Hell.

Whenever you make this type of error, give some money in charity so that the *nafs* feels some sorrow. Additionally, stipulate a penalty of some *rakaʿāt* of *nafl* prayer upon yourself for every error you commit. Stay in the company of honorable and respectable people who do not use this type of speech. Continue beseeching Allah ﷻ for your reformation. By mustering courage and by the blessings of *duʿā*, this sickness will be expelled, Allah willing.

HARSHNESS

The Messenger of Allah ﷺ said, "Allah loves softness and, due to softness, He grants such bounties that He does not grant due to harshness."[51] In another ḥadīth, the Messenger of Allah ﷺ said, "The person who is deprived of softness is deprived of all goodness."[52]

51. Narrated by Muslim on the authority of ʿĀ'isha ﷺ
52. Narrated by Muslim on the authority of Jarīr b. ʿAbdullah ﷺ

NOT FORGIVING PEOPLE'S MISTAKES

This is also a sign of harshness and a hard heart. The Messenger of Allah ﷺ said, "If a person seeks forgiveness from his Muslim brother and the latter does not accept, then let him not come to me at my pond of *Kawthar*." This means that if someone wrongs you and then asks for forgiveness, you should forgive him.

ABSTAINING FROM SPEAKING

The Messenger of Allah ﷺ said, "It is not permissible for a Muslim brother to stop speaking to his Muslim brother for more than three days. If he dies in this condition, he will go to Hell."[53] It should be mentioned, however, that this refers to someone who stops speaking to his brother for some worldly reason rather than religiously justifiable reasons.

PROMISES AND TRUSTS

The Messenger of Allah ﷺ said, "There is no *Imān* (faith) for he who has no *amāna* (trust). There is no religion for the one who does not fulfill his promise."[54]

---

53. Narrated by Abū Dāwūd on the authority of Abū Hurayrah ؓ
54. Narrated by Aḥmad on the authority of Anas b. Mālik ؓ

Conclusion

HERE, THE MAIN EVIL QUALITIES have been mentioned. By the blessings of abstaining from these, all of one's evil qualities and traits will be reformed, Allah-willing.

The Important Advice of Ḥakīm al-Ummah Thānwī ﵀ Regarding One's Shaykh

If a person has, for a considerable period of time, remained in the company of a Shaykh, but has not felt the effect of that company or seen any change, then he should endeavor to seek out the company of a different Shaykh. This is because the actual objective is the Being of Allah ﷻ – not the Shaykh, who is only the means for attaining Allah.

Needless to say, we should not form evil thoughts about our first Shaykh. It may just be possible that he is in fact a *kāmil* (completed) Shaykh and can complete others, but it was just not decreed through him in our case. Similarly, if one's Shaykh passes away before achieving his objective, or if the Shaykh does not give time or attention to his *murīd*, then – accordingly – one can search for a different Shaykh. One should not think, "What is the need for another Shaykh? I will attain *fayḍ* (spiritual blessings) from the grave of my Shaykh." This is because the blessings of the spiritual teachings and reformation cannot occur from the grave.

If a person suffers from misunderstandings or needs to be rectified, know that this rectification can only take place in person through the medium of interaction and in the company of a living Shaykh. If mere spiritual blessings were the purpose of this path, then Allah ﷻ would not have sent living Messengers, in the flesh, to guide and reform mankind and clarify their doubts and misconceptions. Know that it is only a *ṣāḥib al-nisbah*[55] who will continue to can attain progress at this stage.

That said, to leave the Shaykh due to greed, evil thoughts, or even due to the Shaykh's harshness and reprimands is clear deprivation. In such cases, there is a fear of one's connection with Allah ﷻ being severed. Such a person will become

55. A person who has a special connection with Allah Most Exalted.

famous for "jumping on the band-wagon" of many different Shaykhs; hence, he will be deprived of the blessings of the path. May Allah ﷻ grant us sound understanding, humility, and servitude. *Āmīn*!

Since the Shaykh is a complete *Khalīfa* and deputy of the Messenger of Allah ﷺ, one must show him utter love and respect. One should think, "For me, there is no one better, no one who can grant me more benefit, than my spiritual guide." This has been stated by Shaykh Ḥājjī Imdādullāh Muhājir Makkī ؒ.

Finally, I will mention the essence of this path: Whoever does not annihilate his *nafs* (and humble himself) will not attain anything. One will attain the honor of both worlds simply by annihilating one's ego and living with humility and submissiveness. Though Khwāja Ṣāḥib ؒ was a man of great status and honor, he had said to his Shaykh, Ḥakīm al-Ummah Thānwī ؒ:

نہیں کچھ اور خواہش آپ کے در پر لایا ہوں

مٹا دیجے مٹا دیجے میں مٹنے ہی کو آیا ہوں

I have brought only one desire to your door:
Annihilate me, annihilate me,
I have come to be annihilated.

May Allah, Most Exalted, due to His graces, accept this booklet and make it beneficial. *Āmīn*! I request our honorable readers for *duʿās* that Allah, Most Exalted, by His mercy, grant us and all of the readers the ability to practice upon this. *Āmīn*!

(Ḥaḍrat Mawlānā Ḥakīm) Muḥammad Akhtar
(May Allah have mercy on him)
6 *Dhū al-Ḥijja*, 1399 AH